MUSEUMS
and how to use them

MUSEUMS
and how to use them

Eugenie Alexander NDD ATD

B T Batsford Limited

For John

© Eugenie Alexander 1974
First published 1974

ISBN 0 7134 2167 3

Printed in Great Britain by
Bristol Typesetting Co Ltd, Bristol
for the publishers B T Batsford Limited
4 Fitzhardinge Street, London W1H 0AH

Contents

Acknowledgment

My thanks to museum staffs, past pupils and students, teachers (with whom I worked, and those who taught me) for their help and stimulation; also to my family for their encouragement and forbearance while the book was being written; to Liza Vance, who translated my frenzied handwriting into type and to Thelma M. Nye of Batsfords.

London 1974   E A

The author and publishers thank the trustees of the following for permission to reproduce photographs:

The Ashmolean Museum, Oxford for the unglazed horse and figures
   facing pages 61 and 77
The British Museum, London for the onyx offering bowl
The British Museum, Museum of Mankind for figure facing page 60
The National Gallery, London for figure facing page 13
The National Portrait Gallery, London for figures facing pages
   76 and 124
The National Maritime Museum, Greenwich for figures facing pages
   109 and 125
The Science Museum, London for figures facing pages 28, 29
The Tate Gallery for *Recumbent Figure 1938* by Henry Moore
The Victoria and Albert Museum, London for the Goat in white
   porcelain, and figures facing pages 12, 29 (top), 45 and 108
The Wallace Collection for figure facing page 44

Foreword

Over five hundred museums housing selections of exhibits that appeal to boys and girls of all ages have been listed in this book. The National Gallery, the National Portrait Gallery and the Tate Gallery have been included for although they are not museums in the usual sense of the word, the works of art in their collections reflect all aspects of social history, especially fashions in painting, portraiture, and costume, from earliest times to the present day.

In a book of this size it is impossible to cover every museum in Britain and many of the smaller ones are not mentioned. However, these are always worth visiting for their exhibits of local interest. Their addresses can be obtained easily from telephone directories or public libraries in the area.

Many people feel that stronger links could be made between local museums and their schools by organising more competitions and displays by schoolchildren related to the museum exhibits. For example, portraits of famous local people, past and present; flower designs in embroidery based on motifs seen on pottery, tapestry, etc; folk history pamphlets as researched from furniture, utensils, costume, etc; fabric designs for cushions, scarves, and shirts based on patterned objects from Rome, Egypt, China and other countries. Children will gain more from the visual impact of a museum visit than they absorb from hours in the classroom, even with the most imaginative of teachers.

It is hoped that this book will encourage teachers to use their initiative in organising visits that will bring textbooks to life and help children towards a greater understanding, appreciation and recognition of objects and paintings.

1 Introduction

Museums are a valuable teaching aid which is often much neglected, in many cases because little is known about the facilities they provide. Only recently have colleges of education and further training begun to show an awareness of the usefulness of museum visits by offering lectures on how to prepare for and organise them and the best ways to co-operate with museum staff. This book has been compiled with the intention of helping teachers and students – and parents – to make the most of the amenities available. Chapter 3, in which exhibits in a selection of Britain's larger museums are described in some detail, should be particularly useful for teachers in that it offers ideas for follow-up projects involving a wide range of arts and crafts. Other, more general ideas are suggested in chapter 4. Many of these are based on requirements for GCE 'O' and 'A' levels and CSE syllabuses; all are devised to foster an appreciation of shape, colour and texture. Ideas for future topics and projects will often come directly from the class if sufficient interest has been generated by the first visit.

A museum is the finest example of a two- and three-dimensional visual aid. Exhibits can be looked at as links in history, as objects of beauty, of originality, or as parts of a familiar pattern; and while books, films and television are valuable sources of information, they cannot replace the impact of the original. The exciting fact about using such an aid is that through investigating the history of one object or tracing the development of one idea an interest can be aroused in related topics.

Consider, for instance, the tiger. In a zoo we can see a live tiger in his full beauty and observe his appearance, his diet and behaviour in captivity. At the Commonwealth Institute a further study can be made: there is a standing specimen of a tiger from Bengal lurking in the elephant grass on the edge of a village. Details of markings and colourings are more clearly visible, and through the accompanying photographs, models, pictures and film we can learn about the country he came from, the jungle he lived in, his food, his place in the animal kingdom and his treatment by human beings – hunters and game wardens.

There are a number of artists' and craftsmen's interpretations of the tiger and many museums house examples of such work. The British Museum has some on coins, which required a design simple enough for the raised effect and fitting into a circular shape. At the Victoria and

Albert Museum we can find ' Tipu's tiger ', a large working model of a British soldier being mauled by the animal – he cries out when a button is pressed. This is a trophy from the British capture of Mysore in 1799. Also to be seen are small carvings of tigers in wood and ivory, materials which demanded extreme simplicity of line; and, in contrast, Persian paintings of the animal using a flowing, decorative stylisation.

By now the study of a single subject has involved natural history, geography, social history, craftwork and painting. Literature can be included by reading William Blake's *Tyger! Tyger! burning bright in the forests of the night.* With all these ideas in his mind each child should be ready to work out his own interpretation of a tiger, perhaps by designing a woven rug, a fabric collage or a linocut.

Opening up a single topic in this manner is, of course, very much the responsibility of the teacher. While museums are extremely helpful, it is not their policy to usurp the teacher's role. As described in a report on the children's gallery at the Science Museum: ' It is for the schools to teach, for museums to promote a living interest.' After any museum visit some kind of ' follow-up ' at school is important either by discussion, writing, or drawing.

Preliminary visits
Some people go to museums with no clear intention other than to see as much as possible, and wander from room to room trying to absorb everything at once. This can be confusing and exhausting; and it is often more rewarding, particularly for a large group, to make an intensive study of a single section or period. The teacher can best prepare for this by visiting the museum beforehand to look round on his own. Maps of galleries and general information leaflets are usually available at the main entrance and these, coupled with the teacher's own interests, will give some guidance in deciding where to begin. It may be worth buying a separate booklet on the section chosen, as this will provide an introduction to individual exhibits. The map will save endless unnecessary inquiries; but if departments or galleries still prove difficult to find, warders will be on hand to give directions.

School visits
Each child should take with him drawing and writing materials, including a sheet of card on which to rest his paper and suitable pens, pencils and crayons. Visitors are asked to take care that they do not obstruct the view of others while sketching, and not to rest art materials on the plinths, showcases or exhibits. Stools will often be available. In some museums a permit will be required if paints are to be used.

It is helpful to all concerned if children are reminded to treat a museum like a public library: to walk rather than run or skate; to talk

Sketching in the Victoria and Albert Museum, London

Baptism of Christ by Piero della Francesca
Reproduced by courtesy of the Trustees The National Gallery, London

quietly instead of shouting; and, most important, not to touch exhibits unless it is stated that they are allowed to do so. This prohibition includes rails around exhibits and display cases. If the party can be prevented from creating an uproar, warders are more likely to have the energy and inclination to direct streams of small boys to such delights as bloodthirsty weapons, books made from human skin and instruments of incredibly nasty torture.

There are usually cloakrooms for coats and lavatories which should be adequately signposted. It is helpful to cultivate the habit of looking out for signs and reading noticeboards which give details of lectures and films (children are often better at this than adults). Some museums will supply leaflets or news-sheets with this information on request.

With breaks for ' elevenses ' and lunch, older children can manage up to an hour and a half of concentration and true enjoyment in a museum. Some museums have canteens, snack bars or sandwich rooms, mainly for the benefit of children; and although they do not permit eating and drinking anywhere other than in the places provided, those with adjoining gardens usually have some seating accommodation.

If children want to buy postcards or prints, it is suggested that they are taken to the bookstall in small groups rather than all at once.

To save disappointment, it should be borne in mind that not all the exhibits mentioned in this book or in the museum's leaflets will necessarily be on display at the time of a visit; some may be undergoing restoration, others may be out on loan and whole galleries may be closed for alterations.

If the party is on a day excursion it is a good idea to follow the museum visit with a complete change of environment, perhaps by going on to a park where sketches can be made for future work. If the school is visiting a museum nearby, however, a number of short visits can be followed immediately with project work, linked to form a continuous lesson.

2 Information and facilities

It is advisable to check times, days of opening and admission charges (if any) before proposed school visits. In certain museums these must be booked well in advance, as school parties cannot be admitted if the galleries are full.

Education departments

Most of the larger national museums have an education department. Before a visit it is useful to write or go to this department for leaflets and information about its services, which may include such facilities as lectures, clubs, film shows, competitions, intra/extra-mural teaching, and loans. Ask to be put on the mailing list for future exhibitions.

Some museums already have or intend to provide facilities for classes to work inside the building, in the form of store rooms, study sections, display materials, book collections and space for leisure-time activities including craftwork. Certain times are allocated for their use.

Some education departments arrange courses of lessons for children under thirteen, and deal with special requirements for CSE and GCE exams for older pupils. These lessons, which make use of slides, films, gallery exhibits and specimens, are given by experienced qualified teachers, either in the galleries or in the children's centre. They last for 60 to 90 minutes, and time is usually allowed for children to draw the exhibits studied and to do some independent research; their own teacher may be asked to assist here.

On Saturday mornings and during school holidays museum art advisers often run clubs where instruction is given in various crafts. At holiday times, too, adults are offered a wide range of courses, both theoretical and practical, covering such interests as art, architecture and embroidery; and there are lectures and films for children and adults. Some counties are now organising courses on the use of museums in teaching – student teachers should apply for these through their colleges. All other applications, and requests for information and film tickets, can be made directly to the education department of the museum concerned. The department will also reserve tables in the museum's restaurant or snack bar for visiting school parties.

A museum guide or lecturer can be provided for a school visit if plenty of notice is given to the education officer. Some places, such as the

Natural History and Science Museums in London, need up to a term's notice; others require at least a month. When arranging this the teacher can help to ensure the success of the visit by supplying the following information:

(a) the sex and approximate age group of the children
(b) the type of school and educational level
(c) the number of pupils in the group
(d) the subject the children are studying
(e) how the class is being prepared for the visit
(f) the teacher's method of approaching the subject
(g) what they hope to see during the visit and learn from it
(h) confirmation that the teacher accepts responsibility for discipline.

The ideal number for a school party is twenty children per teacher. Teachers have been known to turn up with a hundred pupils, knowing that the rooms are large; and while it is possible for a group of this size to look at the elephants in the central hall of the Natural History Museum, chaos will ensue when the dormouse is reached.

Another responsibility of education departments is the provision of special facilities for handicapped children. Wheelchairs are sometimes available and there may be a supply of objects which can be used by blind children to develop their sense of textures and shapes through touch. Booklets for young children containing information and quizzes about exhibits are issued by some departments.

Children often write to education departments with questions whose answers could easily be found in their school or public library, and this should not be encouraged. If specialised information is required, however, museums will supply it or suggest a reading list, although some take several weeks to answer such inquiries.

Temporary exhibitions

It is a good idea to look out for unusual, exciting, well-displayed and instructive temporary exhibitions. These usually last for six weeks or three months, and a tremendous amount of work goes into their preparation. After the initial conception there is the collection of exhibits, involving letters and visits to staff in other museums and public and private owners; then transportation and unpacking must be organised and suitable display cases, stands and lighting acquired; and finally special posters, labels, catalogues and invitation cards must be written, designed and printed, and adequate press coverage ensured.

It is interesting, on these occasions, to see how items borrowed from other museums often take on a new look in a different setting.

Here are some examples of successful temporary exhibitions which have been held in the past.

The British in India   Brighton Museum and Art Gallery

A nostalgic re-creation of a vanished era, sponsored by the Brighton Festival Society. Exhibits included a delightful gouache, ' Lady Impey in her boudoir examining her hat [just handed to her by the milliner] while supervising her household '; a richly carved ivory throne decorated with lions and emblems, and other treasures from the Royal Collections; Mughal miniatures; a mosquito net (specially obtained from India); a furnished room; costumes; old photographs projected on a screen; the call of a mynah bird, elephants trumpeting and other typical Indian sounds on tape. The festival was opened by Earl Mountbatten of Burma (the last Viceroy of India) with the 10th Gurkha Rifles playing the pipes and drums.

Treasures of Tutankhamun   British Museum, London

A superb collection of furniture, sculpture and jewellery from the tomb of an Egyptian pharaoh of the 18th dynasty (*c* 1350 BC), which was discovered, with the mummy intact, in 1922.

Scientific Toys   Science Museum, London

It is now widely accepted that the best toys are made from harmless materials imaginatively and safely adapted to a child's age in such a way that he develops his manual skills and reasoning powers through play. This exhibition consisted entirely of toys which demonstrated scientific principles or encouraged the development of skills, from many different periods in history.

The Elizabethan Image   Tate Gallery, London

A display covering the history of painting and costume and styles in English portraiture during the seventy-five years from the death of Holbein to the arrival of Van Dyck. The Friends of the Tate Society organised an evening party during the exhibition with Elizabethan food, costume and music.

The Craftman's Art   Victoria and Albert Museum, London

A collection of exhibits which included jewellery, pottery, weaving, embroidery, collages and glassware designed and made by some of the leading contemporary craftsmen living in Britain. It would be interesting to know how many of these will be museum pieces in 100 years' time.

Loan collections and outside lectures

Some museums have circulation departments which lend exhibits to other museums, colleges, schools and societies. Museum staff may be prepared to visit schools and adult societies to give lectures illustrated with colour slides and possibly objects from their reserve collections.

Libraries
Users of museum libraries will sometimes be required to give a signature, fill in a form with details of the title, author and publisher of the book they wish to consult, or apply for a special ticket for research. Advice can be obtained about the best books on certain subjects and use of the catalogue for various projects. There is often a separate children's section.

Written inquiries
Adults with queries concerning, for example, the genuineness, period or identity (but not value) of objects should write to the head of the appropriate department enclosing a stamped addressed envelope. If photographs are sent they should be clear.

Information about famous people, objects and dates can be obtained by colleges, schools and private individuals. It is advisable to make an appointment to consult a member of staff.

Teachers, parents or children with suggestions about the museum itself should write to the secretary or the education officer.

Sales
Most large museums have a sales department, usually situated near the main entrance, which stocks guide books, specialised catalogues, books on exhibited collections, large reproductions of pictures, slides, postcards and Christmas cards in season, and where questions about the size and cost of photographs are answered. If photographs are required it is best to place a written order with the sales or publications department and pay in advance (including the cost of postage). If negatives are already available the prints should arrive fairly rapidly; otherwise there will be a delay while a special photograph is taken, and the cost will be higher. Some museums permit visitors to take their own photographs, particularly the smaller museums which do not have resident photographers.

Associations
Some museums have associations which charge a fee for membership; members are entitled to attend private views of exhibitions and evening parties, and can obtain reductions in fees for cultural visits at home and abroad. There are also young people's associations for various age groups.

The Contemporary Art Society and the National Art Collections Fund lend their support to museums and art galleries.

A glance behind the scenes
Not everything that goes on in museums is open to the public gaze. The activities of the conservation department, for example, are usually taken for granted, yet they are of the greatest importance in prolonging the lives and maintaining the quality of exhibits. Paintings must be cleaned,

perhaps re-lined, and X-rayed – sometimes with exciting results; sculpture may have been dismantled for transportation and will have to be reassembled on arrival; pottery needs mending; furs, feathers and fabrics require immunisation against moths, paper against insects, bronzes against green discoloration; pieces from natural history and science sections must be wired and have any missing parts replaced. Attached to the department are laboratories where powdered dyes from vegetables, fruits and earths are kept in test-tubes for comparison with colours used hundreds of years ago on pottery, paintings and textiles.

In all departments records must be kept up to date and new acquisitions researched. Labels have to be replaced, perhaps redesigned, new pamphlets must be written, the supply of bookstall material maintained and endless questions answered.

In many large and small museums the imaginative and fitting display of objects indicate the staff's appreciation of art and design. However intelligent and attentive the visitor, he tends to tire easily and absorb very little of what he sees if the display is poorly designed. Wall colourings and textures, cases and stands, wood, glass, fabric, paint and paper placed behind or beneath exhibits all play a part in giving ease and enjoyment to viewing. Attention must be paid to proportion, size, texture and colour in an arrangement. Labels are often ignored, or have poor lettering, badly spaced and placed. Lighting may detract where it should subtly emphasise.

Good design in books, pamphlets, posters and other material produced by museums is equally important for stimulating interest and making an impact. A number of museums were asked to provide information for this book, and readily obliged.

3 The larger museums

The museums and art galleries selected for detailed treatment in this chapter house between them almost every kind of exhibition that can be found in museums throughout the world and, on a smaller scale, elsewhere in Britain.

The projects suggested for following up a visit to each museum can easily be adapted for use in relation to any other. It is a good idea to give a list of these to the children in advance so that they can make notes during the visit. Some will require an introductory talk by the teacher and background material will be found among the books listed on pages 151-2.

Museums providing services and loans are indicated as follows:
*   services; loans to city or area;
Δ   services only.
For further information about services and loans see chapter 5.

ENGLAND

BIRMINGHAM CITY MUSEUM AND ART GALLERY
Congreve Street, Birmingham 3

Department of art: fine collection of Old Master paintings, English watercolours, sculpture, ceramics and silver. Archaeology: exhibits from Greece, Egypt, India, China, Persia, Central and Southern America, including glass, jewellery and pottery. Natural history: birds, animal life on land and in the water, skeletons and skulls.
*   Apply to Schools Liaison Officer   Competitions and other activities arranged for the holidays

Some exhibits in Birmingham Museum and Art Gallery
Horned dinosaur skull
Fossilised relic of the horned dinosaur Triceratops, which roamed North America 90 million years ago.

Paintings by David Cox (1783–1859)
Born in Birmingham. Renowned for his landscape watercolours. He accidentally discovered a new kind of paper in Dundee and something

similar is now sold as 'Cox' paper. It is rough, slightly tinted, and absorbs colour washes of paint quickly. His effects are broad and vigorous with the freshness and transparency which is the essence of the water-colour medium.

Copper Buddha from Bengal

This is a unique survival from the large-scale metal statuary made around AD 400. Buddha means 'the Awakened' or 'the Enlightened' and the one Buddha (or holy man) known to history was Siddharta, a prince who lived somewhere between Benares and Nepal 2000 years ago. Ceylon, Burma, Siam, Tibet, China and Japan have all been influenced in their history and culture by the followers of Buddha.

The Evans stamp collection

44 000 stamps in a representative selection of the world's issues from 1840 to 1938. An instructive display which demonstrates the colour and design achievements of many different countries.

Gallery of British birds

Displays are arranged in simulated natural surroundings and show parent birds with their nests and young. Visitors can listen to recordings of the birdsongs most commonly heard in the Midlands.

Ideas for classwork based on visits to the Birmingham City Museum and Art Gallery

1   You are starting a small fine art gallery and plan to specialise in either (a) the Pre-Raphaelites or (b) nineteenth-century British watercolours. *Any* pictures in either of these categories can be borrowed for the opening exhibition – this would be a miracle but imagine it is so. With the help of postcards, cuttings and sketches, design a catalogue with (a) a cover bearing the title of the exhibition, (b) brief biographies of three of the artists, (c) a reproduction of one picture by each of them, (d) a short autobiography of the dealer (ie yourself), stating your qualifications, knowledge of the history of art, and so on – this can be invented, (e) information about the name, address and opening times of the gallery and duration of the exhibition.

You are giving a 'private view' party for this opening. Make a list of ten guests (including eminent local people) and choose someone to declare the exhibition open.

2   A mammal, a bird and a fish are discussing and contrasting their homes. Find examples of these animals and the places where they live. Give an account of each one, making drawings. Which kind of home would you prefer to have and why?

3   In the museum pamphlet just above the heading 'Archaeology', there is a fascinating picture of an object which appears to be half-clown, half-

animal. What do you think it is? Which country is it from? What medium do you think it is made in, what colour is it and how big? Find it in the museum and discover how near you were to the truth.

4 Paint a picture of one of the gay, decorated barges that were once a feature of our waterways. It is early morning: what birds and animals can be seen among the reeds, trees and flowers? Look round the natural history and botanical sections of the museum, which should give you some ideas.

5 Look at the medals and coins. Design a badge, using an appropriate animal, for two of the following: (a) a swimmer, (b) a footballer, (c) a cricketer, (d) a speedway rider.

6 Compare the works of three present-day sculptors with three from the past, choosing one work by each and commenting in each case on (a) the medium used, (b) the handling of the medium, (c) the subject chosen, (d) the concept (figurative, abstract, romantic or classical). Who is your favourite sculptor and why?

7 Choose one favourite item from each of the following sections, describe it, outline its history and say why you like it: (a) pottery, (b) jewellery, (c) glasswork.

8 Study some of the information in the natural history section of the museum, then describe as factually as possible a day in the life of your pet (which can be an imaginary one) as experienced by the animal. The museum pamphlet dealing with ' bird folklore ' might help towards some unusual ideas.

9 The museum has a large and varied collection of weapons, domestic equipment, tools and *objets d'art* from the ancient cultures of Central and South America. Choose six such items and imagine they all belonged to a family living in those times. Make up a story about the objects you have selected and the family, describing also their clothes, home, surroundings and climate.

10 Watch two pidgeons, cats, dogs, fish, or insects together, study designs of them in the museum. Look at Picasso's pictures showing a cockerel or person with the frontal and side views expressed in one and the same face. (Find these in a book in your local library.) Using this method, choose your favourite animal, and make a machine or hand embroidered picture or one with felt tips, ink, or paint, or try out this idea in modelling clay.

BRISTOL CITY MUSEUM AND ART GALLERY
Queen's Road, Bristol 8

Paintings and sculpture. Classical and British archaeology. Ethnography. Natural history. Geology. Ceramics. Embroidery. Glass.
* *Apply to the Schools' Organiser.* Holiday competitions. Saturday morning club.

Some exhibits in the Bristol City Museum and Art Gallery

' Oliver Cromwell ' privateer glass
Glass goblet made in Bristol to celebrate the commissioning of armed merchant vessels in the Seven Years' War (1756–63), 15 cm (6 in) high with an enamel twist stem and a conical bowl. Engraved ship and lettered design on bowl.

Paintings by Eugène Boudin (1824–98)
Eugène Boudin was born at Honfleur, and was the son of a pilot. A forerunner of Impressionism, he painted beautiful luminous skies, seascapes, harbour and beach scenes with charming figures, bathing huts and umbrellas. There are several excellent ship pictures and a rare example of a still-life by this artist in the gallery.

Bronze head from Benin, West Africa
A compelling exhibit. Textures of hair, latticed hat shape, flowers, and bands round the neck similar to the bangles worn by ' giraffe-necked ' women to elongate their necks, thus increasing their beauty in the eyes of their compatriots.

Bronze sculpture ' Help ' by Bernard Meadows (1915–)
Bernard Meadows is an abstract artist with a strong expressionist side to his work. His bird and crab sculptures convey the feelings of fear, menace, panic and hysteria which everyone has experienced in varying degrees in times of war and stress. This abstract bronze sculpture composed of a related hammer shape, section of a circle and rectangle contains elements of humour, tragedy and oppression. Bronze can be treated in various ways, giving finishes that are bronze-gold, greenish, dark or light.

Model of steamship Great Britain
Long ago ship models were made to scale as a guide to the ship builders. The designer of the *Great Britain* was I. K. Brunel and the ship was built at Bristol in 1843. The partly restored ship (brought over from the Falkland Isles) is now in the dock in which it was originally built.

Giant Irish deer skeleton
A fascinating exhibit – the slim legs, rounded body and giant antlers demonstrate one of nature's most amazing feats of balance and construction.

Some ideas for classwork based on visits to Bristol City Museum and Art Gallery

1 Find as many exhibits as possible connected with one of the following: (a) the horse, (b) the cat, (c) the owl. Search through all the dif-

ferent sections, and look out particularly for plates, textiles and paintings which use the chosen animal or bird as a design motif.

2 Make caricatures or papier mâché models of three of the animals in the natural history section. Choose animals which have a naturally exaggerated feature, such as the giraffe, the rhinoceros and the ostrich.

3 You have been commissioned to make a booklet using twelve motifs from the museum. Make sketches for designs, to be worked out when you are back at school, based on an example of each of the following: (1) tapestry, (2) batik, (3) rugs, (4) carving, (5) plates, (6) silver, (7) vases, (8) clocks, (9) boxes, (10) jewellery, (11) glass, (12) pottery figures. Design a cover with the name of the museum and three of the motifs arranged on it.

4 Pick your favourite exhibit from each of the following countries and make a booklet containing a description and a picture of each one: (a) China, (b) England, (c) India, (d) Africa.

5 You have been commissioned to design a motif for packaging one of the following: (a) Lotus sweets, (b) Lyre honey, (c) Somerset garden perfume, (d) Jungle Fantasy after-shave lotion. Ideas for this can be found in the archaeology, botany or natural history section of the museum. The product is also to be advertised on television. How would you visualise the presentation? Discuss this or write down your ideas.

6 Each of the following passages or poems mentions one or more objects that can be seen in the museum. Choose one, read it in full and illustrate it using a museum exhibit as a model.

(a)   Like as the waves make towards the *pebbled* shore . . .
      (Shakespeare, *Sonnets*, 60)

(b)   Full fathom five thy father lies;
      Of his bones are *coral* made:
      Those are *pearls* that were his eyes . . .
      (Shakespeare, *The Tempest*, I, ii, 394)

(c)   Call for the *robin redbreast* and the *wren* . . .
      (Webster, *The White Devil*, V, iv, 100)

(d)   What was he doing, the great god Pan . . .
      Splashing and paddling with hoof of a *goat*,
      And breaking the golden *lilies* afloat
      With the *dragon-fly* on the river.
      (Elizabeth Barrett Browning, *A Musical Instrument*)

7 In a fantasy story imagine that either a Chinese or an Indian woman from long ago comes across the caravan which is in this museum and decides to take a holiday in it. Illustrate your story with a picture of the woman in the correct costume, the cooking utensils she would use, and all the other furnishing and decorative objects she would take with her. Contrast this form of travel with the type she has been accustomed to.

Remember the landscape she will be in – will it be Chinese, Indian, or English? All this will help with ideas for the story. Objects in the museum will help with the drawings.

8   If you could choose three pictures by British artists and three by French artists for reproduction as prints to hang on your wall, which ones would you pick and why? Give the title of each painting, the artist's name and the date.

9   Choose a piece of embroidery design and make a sketch and show how it could be used for a greetings card.

10   Find a painting which you like by a local artist. Describe it, give the title and write a short biography of the artist. Why does the picture appeal to you?

11   There is to be a television programme showing aspects of Bristol, to be filmed at the museum. Which objects would you choose to illustrate one of the following subjects: (a) the countryside near Bristol, (b) shipping, (c) glass. How would you set about making the film?

BRITISH MUSEUM   Great Russell Street, WC1

Permanent collection of archaeology. Egyptian, British, Greek, Roman, Oriental and Western Asiatic antiquities. Watches and clocks. Coins and medals. Prints and drawings, many by famous artists. Library, to which practically every book published in Great Britain is sent; comprehensive collection of pamphlets and periodicals; also National Collection of Newspapers at the British Museum Newspaper Library, Colindale NW9 (daily and weekly periodicals since 1800).
Δ   *Apply to Education Officer.*

Reading room
Tickets issued to serious students over 21 who cannot find information elsewhere. *Apply to Director's Office.*

Museum of Mankind (Department of Ethnography)
6 Burlington Gardens, W1
This museum has several exhibitions on view, each one is based on a different subject or culture and remains on display for a year. Exhibits include masks, head-dresses, carvings, arms, musical instruments, jewellery and stylised animals.

Some exhibits in the British Museum
Assyrian sculpture
Giant two- and three-dimensional wall panels showing a king in his chariot hunting lions and the Assyrian army with battering rams on wheels. Human-headed, bearded, winged lions from the palace of Ashurna

Sirpal II, and bulls of similar design which were placed at temple entrances to keep away evil spirits.

Egyptian exhibits

' Ginger ', the gruesome mummy, lies on his side in an open wooden box and is a very popular exhibit. Mummy cases. Embalmed cats. Model boats. Hieroglyphics. Painted faces, frontal eye view on side face (Picasso used this convention). Necklaces, amulets and ear-rings.

The goat in the thicket

Head-dress of gold, lapis lazuli and carnelian, 2500 BC, of symbolic, probably mythological significance. Face and legs of gold leaf, horns and shoulder fleece of white shell. Gold leaf for the Sacred Tree came from the Great Death-pit at Ur, city of the ancient Sumerians.

Anglo-Saxon collection

Treasures from the Sutton Hoo burial ship: helmets, cooking pots, bronze shields, broaches and coins. Lindisfarne gospels.

Celtic horned helmet

The only known example of a ritual battle head-dress, found in the Thames at Waterloo Bridge. The ornamentation consists of bronze studs in criss-cross formation enclosing red enamel and a relief design on the front and back.

Greek exhibits

Panels which formed a frieze round the temple of the goddess Athena. Marble friezes from the Parthenon in Athens (collected by Lord Elgin). Decorative bulls, horses and girls with sacrificial vessels. Tanagra figures. Mosaics. Vases. Bronze figure of a warrior on horseback from Lucania.

Chinese exhibits

Camels, horses and dragons in porcelain and jade. Lacquer work. Vases.

Indian section

Statues of gods, including the many-armed Shiva. Cave paintings. Head-dresses.

The Rosetta Stone

Found by Napoleon's army at Rosetta, Egypt, in 1799. A piece of black basalt about 1 metre (3 ft) long on which is written a decree of Ptolomy Epiphanes, c 195 BC, in hieroglyphic (used by priests), demotic (used for legal documents) and Greek characters. The stone enabled scholars to decipher hieroglyphic writing for the first time.

Millefiori glass bowl

The name means 'a thousand flowers' and refers to a technique (often seen in paperweights) which was created originally by the Romans. Flowers constructed from tiny sections of coloured rod are embedded in clear glass. This blue, green, yellow and sepia bowl came from Alexandria.

Ideas for classwork based on visits to the British Museum

1 Coins and medals are sometimes the only record we have of the faces of famous people from the past and their achievements. Find some of these in the museum and make a portrait, inside a circle, based on one of the medals. Find out all you can about the person you have depicted and write about him or her underneath the picture.

2 Study African masks and head-dresses. Make one from papier mâché or cardboard and decorate it with straws, beads, coloured paper and strips of rag stuck on with glue or Sellotape.

3 The pictures on Greek vases are often of real or legendary historical characters; for instance, Bacchus in the woods, Penelope with her loom, Orpheus and his lyre, Croesus on his funeral pyre. Make a list of the stories you can find illustrated in this museum and try to discover more about the characters involved. Draw, or paint on a piece of pottery, a design to represent any story or legend you choose (from any country).

4 Find examples, from three different countries and in three different media, of each of the following: (a) cats, (b) birds, (c) lions. Sketch them all; then choose one animal or bird and make it the subject of a coloured drawing, a painting or a fabric collage, placing it in what you imagine to be its natural setting.

5 Egyptian, African and Assyrian sculptures often feature simple patterned necklaces. Draw one you have seen in the museum that particularly appeals to you and use the pattern in a design for the cover of a needlework case, suitable for embroidering or decorating with bead work and sequins.

6 Buy a black and white postcard of a coin or shield in the museum, cut away the background and place it inside one of the following shapes: (a) a pointed cross, (b) a seven-pointed star, (c) a hexagon, (d) an equilateral triangle. Make a three-coloured patterned design, in keeping with the motif, inside the shapes that are left.

7 Write an essay entitled 'On discovering a wall-painting/plaque', set in one of the following: (a) the Ajanta caves, (b) the desert, (c) Greece, (d) an Egyptian tomb. Was it in daylight or were lamps or candles used to see the pictures or plaque? Were they partly covered in dust or well-preserved? What materials had been used? What story did the pictures depict?

8 Many coins a thousand years old or more depict animals, possibly because they were regarded as sacred at the time. Later, gods, heroes and

kings were also used. Find coins showing some of the following: (a) elephant, Ceylon, (b) bird of paradise, New Guinea, (c) hog, Bermuda, (d) owl, Ancient Greece, (e) lion, East Indian Mohur, (f) tortoise, Early Greece. Sketch your favourite and adapt it for a design for a batik, silk screen or collage.

9   Look for designs on Greek vases illustrating the story of (a) Acis and Galatea or (b) Dido and Aeneas. Read the Greek stories about them, either before or after you visit the museum, and then listen to the operas of these names. Which did you find created the best atmosphere, the music or the book? Do a painting of an incident from one of these myths.

10   Design a case for a mummy (the body of a king, an artist or a musician), using Egyptian patterns, symbols and traditional colours. The most successful designs can be cut out and made into a frieze.

11   Look at the simplified and decorative treatment of faces in Egyptian, Persian and Assyrian portraiture. Base a design for a fabric collage on one of these styles and use a mixture of coloured strings, bottle tops, beads, buttons and sequins for the head-dresses.

12   Model a small plate or bowl from clay and decorate it with pieces of coloured glass or tile, basing the design on the millefiori glass bowl from Alexandria.

13   Study the Greek tanagra figures, particularly the portrayal of drapery, and model a ' mother and child ' or ' father and child ' after that style.

14   Imagine that advertising existed in early Greek, Roman, Indian, Egyptian and Chinese times. Use an appropriately stylised bird, animal or human motif from three of these civilisations to design (a) a poster advertising a certain food, (b) a leaflet showing the latest fashions in clothes or jewellery and (c) a party invitation.

15   Design a calendar which would interest children, basing the illustrations on (1) a woodcut, (2) an Egyptian fresco, (3) Assyrian sculpture, (4) a food or drink container, (5) jewellery, (6) a head-dress, (7) pottery, (8) a mask, (9) an Indian god or goddess, (10) an illustrated manuscript, (11) a Greek horse and rider, (12) a Chinese or Japanese painting. The best design in each section can be cut out and mounted, the days of the month added and the twelve sections assembled as a calendar for classroom use.

COMMONWEALTH INSTITUTE   Kensington High Street, W8

The Institute has been described as ' the Commonwealth under one roof '. Displays illustrate the lives, scenery and resources of Commonwealth peoples including their food, homes, furniture, costume, work, crafts, animals, and climatic conditions. Art gallery shows loan exhibitions, contemporary painting, sculpture and craft work from the Commonwealth.

* *Apply to Chief Education Officer.* Work sheets and quizzes. Children's centre. Cinema. Theatre. Library which lends books and study material. Short courses for teachers (it is hoped to broaden these to include student teachers of painting, sculpture and crafts).

Some exhibits in the Commonwealth Institute

Each member country or state has a section which contains some of the following exhibits:

(a) An object which is easily recognised as being representative of its country or state of origin. Ceylon, for example, has a large reproduction of a statue of Buddha.

(b) A typical landscape in the form of a diorama.

(c) Large and small models of people in typical costume, houses and temples, animals, birds and fish.

(d) Objects such as drums, puppets, masks and carvings representing the cultural life of the area.

(e) Exhibits showing the geography, industry, education, health, food and social history of the place.

Singapore

The section contains a relief model of the island, a three-dimensional panoramic view, butterfly specimens against typical scenery with artificial flowers and foliage, a tank of live tropical fish, a rubber tree with seeds, coral and a spray of orchids. Models include Sir Stamford Raffles (the founder of Singapore), nineteenth-century merchants and a trading steamer from that period. Photographs and recordings describe the people and their lives, trades and houses. Colour transparencies set in a large revolving drum depict aspects of modern Singapore.

Durga

Durga was one of the forms of Devi, the mother goddess. A large figure, once used in a Hindu festival, made from pith and decorated with tinsel and coloured foil. She is seated on the lion that carried her into battle when she rescued the universe from evil by killing Mahishasura, the buffalo demon.

Carpet weaving (India)

Diorama of a typical family carpet-weaving business in a yard leading off a Punjab city street. The weavers sit in a row in front of the loom. Various workers are preparing the raw wool, winding it round a spool and dyeing it.

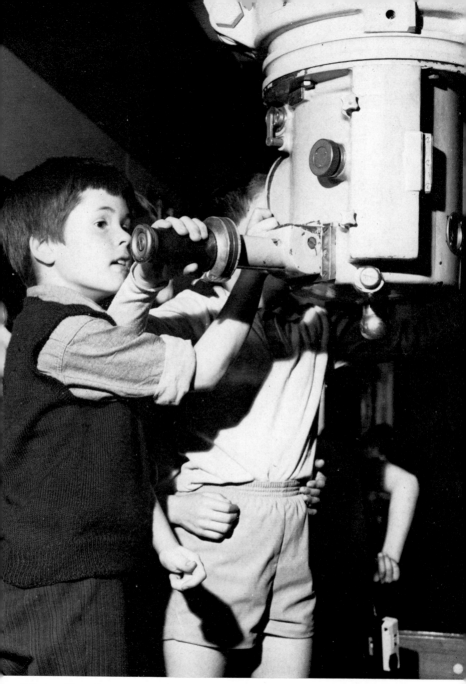

The working of a periscope holds the interest of small boys in the Children's Gallery
Crown copyright   Science Museum, London

Studying the beautiful inlaid decoration on the butt of rifles in the Victoria and Albert Museum, London

Aveling and Porter traction engine, 1871
Crown copyright   Science Museum, London

Festival dragon (Hong Kong)
A huge colourful patterned dragon breathing out a ball of fire, embellished with silks, sequins and different types of thread.

Silver barge (Brunei)
A silver casket in the shape of a royal barge, on a silver stand, which was presented to Her Majesty Queen Elizabeth II when she visited the country in 1953.

Vorura beaded crown
A head-dress made entirely of different shaped beads, with three-dimensional birds encircling the top, a decorative head-piece (with faces and abstract patterns on it) and, beneath this, long strings of small beads hanging in a circle.

Ideas for classwork based on visits to the Commonwealth Institute
1 Choose a single section, look at all the exhibits it contains and make a pamphlet about the country with a page on each of the following: (1) scenery, (2) climate, (3) people in national dress, (4) homes, (5) animals, (6) work, (7) crafts, (8) food. Each page should carry a picture as well as writing. Design a cover which sums up the people and the land they live in.
2 Make clay models of one or two people from a selected country and construct a cardboard model of their home.
3 Look for representations of the dragon (a mythological creature) in the museum and make a three-dimensional one from coloured paper and tissues.
4 Sketch three examples of designs embroidered on clothes or articles. Make notes on the colours, types of thread and beads or sequins which have been used. Make something in the embroidery class using an idea from one of the designs.
5 Divide the class into six groups with at least one good artist in each. Choose a different country for each group and assign individual members to study and sketch the following: (a) people and costume, (b) food, (c) landscape, (d) homes, (e) crafts or work, (f) animals. Each group can then make a large painting or paper collage to represent the country chosen. Discuss colours and general composition.
6 If there is a craft exhibition in the art gallery at the time of your visit, sketch one of the following and find a similar item elsewhere in the museum to sketch beside it: (a) a pot, (b) a plate, (c) a hanging or embroidery, (d) a small piece of wooden sculpture, (e) something made of glass. Make notes and comments on the colours and materials used, and say which of the two you prefer and why.
7 Make a six-page pamphlet about fruit for a greengrocer's shop. Do a

c

painting or paper collage of a different fruit for each page, and say where it comes from. Design a cover with a basket or bowl containing all six fruits.

8   Make coloured drawings using pen and ink and felt pens or coloured pencils of three of the following in national dress: (a) a Dyak woman, (b) an Iban of Borneo, (c) a Tonga belle, (d) a Fiji chief, (e) a Kandyan chief, (f) a woman from Burma, (g) a Samoan warrior, (h) a Dominican woman.

9   Make a four-page travel leaflet encouraging people to visit any country you choose. Advertise the attractions of the place, such as sunshine, blue water, charming people, good food, opportunities for recreation and anything else you can think of. The cover should have the name of the country on it and be designed in such a way that people want to open it and look inside for further information.

10   The Commonwealth Institute museum was opened in November 1962 by Her Majesty Queen Elizabeth II. Comment on your impressions of the building, including the external architecture and the unusual ceiling and arrangement of staircases inside.

11   What is the Commonwealth? How many countries belong to it? Name six, and choose one to write about and illustrate under the following headings: (a) food, (b) social and working lives of the people, (c) climate, (d) housing.

12   What are the countries of origin for rubber, aluminium, asbestos, jute, uranium and what are their main uses? Make an abstract picture including these textures.

13   Sketch the man's helmet from Ghana and compare it with one of the following from another museum: (a) a Viking's helmet, (b) a Roundhead's helmet, (c) an English or German helmet worn in the first world war. Write a story about a dramatic event in the life of one of the wearers.

14   Look round the Commonwealth Institute and design one of the following, basing your idea on a similar article: (a) a hat for Ascot, (b) a costume for the beach, (c) a gala gown.

15   Make a mask, basing the design on one seen in the museum and using some of the following materials: cardboard, paper, fabric, wool, beads, sequins.

16   From one of the countries shown in the museum choose a representative motif (realistic or abstract). Adapt this to a design for a scarf made in batik, silk screen, or linoprint.

GEOLOGICAL MUSEUM   Exhibition Road, South Kensington, SW7

Rock formations, fossils and different features of soils. Minerals and gems, including those put to industrial use. Revolving globe 1.82 m (6 ft)

in diameter. Earthquakes, glaciers and volcanoes. Dioramas of past and present scenes of geological interest. Films.
Δ *Apply to Museum Lecturer.*

Some exhibits in the Geological Museum
Textures in the weathering of sandstones and shales
Weathering of Septarian nodule (locality unknown). The clay has been removed by weathering, leaving the septa of pyrites which resembles the moulding of a honeycomb. Weathered quartzite (locality Sutherland). Specimen of ' piped ' quartzite, a metamorphic rock derived from sandstone with worm burrows; the pipes have eroded more slowly than the matrix.

Differential weathering (locality India). Agate on which the softest bands have been quickly and easily eroded.

Pele's hair
Fine threads and hairs of glossy lava formed by the action of strong wind on a fountain of very liquid lava in Kilauea, Hawaii.

Coal
Long ago Britain was a tropical country and where there are now beds of coal there once grew swampy forests of giant ferns, reeds and similar plants. The history of coal and the different types that have been found can be studied in the museum.

Shells and fossils
Freshwater shells found in rocks and sand show that Britain was once a part of the landmass of Europe and South-East England formed the delta of a great Continental river. Fossilised bones provide evidence that animals which flourish in tropical countries – elephants, rhinoceroses, crocodiles and tigers – once roamed over Britain. (These animals can be seen in the Natural History Museum.)

Earthquakes and volcanoes
The displacement of rock strata, so that layers of a certain rock are near the surface in one district and more deeply buried nearby, is proof of a great upheaval or earthquake at some time in history. Ancient beds of lava on Snowdon and in other areas show that Britain once had many fierce and active volcanoes.

Precious stones and minerals
These come from Britain and many other countries including India, Australia and New Zealand. Some of the most beautifully coloured

examples are onyx (Scotland), chessylite (New South Wales), labradorite (Labrador), fluorspar (Canada) and galena (Nigeria).

Rocks and pebbles
After failing to find information in books on the subject, hundreds of adults and children take their holiday collections of rocks and pebbles to the museum to identify them. No self-respecting collector would dream of asking for professional advice unless he had looked at every item on display and found nothing similar.

Ideas for classwork based on visits to the Geological Museum
1   Paint a grotto in which there are stalactites and stalagmites, rocks (study the colours in the museum) and an underground stream. Try to achieve rough, smooth, watery and rocky textures.

2   Look at some crystals, for example semi-transparent calcite, or fossil sea-urchins found in chalk; use the most attractive shape and pattern for a ' repeat' abstract design for wallpaper. For which room in a house or flat would it be most suitable?

3   Select one of the carboniferous plants in the museum and use it as the basis for a machined fabric collage or embroidery design.

4   After studying the museum displays, find out all you can about the soil in your area or garden. Draw a plan indicating the various substances it contains.

5   Construct a model of a river, lake or stream; include rocks and mountains or perhaps a hill with grass and trees. Glass, pebbles, cauliflower tops, crinkled wire and pieces of carpet are some of the materials you may find useful.

6   Paint a picture of the eruption of Vesuvius, complete with people and nearby houses.

7   Describe and illustrate an example of each of the following, and say where it can be found: (a) clay, (b) chalk, (c) redrock, (d) limestone.

8   Design a four-coloured rug using the shapes of deposits found in the Fens. Perhaps this could be woven by some of the class.

9   Much of our knowledge of ancient history comes from the study of rocks and fossils. Imagine you have found a tooth, a broken skull, a fossilised plant and a small animal's skeleton. Draw these, explain what forms of life you think they came from and write a story in which they feature.

10   The sculptor Henry Moore picks up pebbles on the beach and these often stimulate certain ideas in his mind. Try to find some interesting pebbles while you are on holiday and take them back to school for an *objet trouvé* collection.

11   Rubies and sapphires, both of which come from the mineral corundum, can be found in several different forms and colours. Describe some

of these, decide which colour and texture you like best and say what kind of jewellery you would make from it. What substance would you use for the setting? Would there be any additional decoration? Make a sketch of the proposed design.

12   Sometimes similar patterns, for instance the one which resembles honeycomb moulding, can be found in different textured rocks. Draw four of these patterns and say in what types of rock they can be found.

13   In what ways are the industry and agriculture of a country influenced by its soils, minerals and rocks? Answer this question in relation to part of one of the following areas: the British Isles, Europe, North and South America, Africa, India, Australia and New Zealand.

14   Look at the following substances, and describe one object that you have seen made from each: (a) iron, (b) clay, (c) aluminium, (d) zinc.

15   Design and write an illustrated six-page booklet on ' The History of the Moon ' from the aspect that interests you most. Describe its composition as you understand it.

16   Look at as many different pieces of rock as possible and at models of hills and mountains in different countries. Either make and paint your own model, or paint a picture showing the different textures where grass or heather softens the outline of the bare rock. Say where your hill or mountain might be found.

IMPERIAL WAR MUSEUM   Lambeth Road, SE1

History of two world wars. Original aircraft and weapons, including tanks and a doodle bug. Model ships. Uniforms. Diorama of the Battle of Taranto, 1940, with a push-button for night or day. Spy section. Overlord Embroidery, 80.5 m (264 ft) long, designed in 33 panels and commissioned from the Royal School of Needlework: tells the story of the D-Day invasion of Normandy. This is 10 m (33 ft) longer than the Bayeux Tapestry. Pictures by war artists, including Edward Ardizzone: ' Looting from a Disabled Truck ', Henry Moore; ' Women and Children in the Tube ', Paul Nash: ' Battle of Britain ', Stanley Spencer: ' Travoys '.

Δ *Apply to Educational Department*   Questionnaires for school children of all ages. Cinema: films about the two world wars for juniors, teenagers and college students.

Some exhibits in the Imperial War Museum
Old Fred
An Avro Lancaster B1 heavy bomber, decorated with an inaccurately reproduced Australian flag and an animal cartoon. A platform enables visitors to look inside the cockpit.

Autograph book with signatures of the ' few '
' Never was so much owed by so many to so few ' – Churchill's words
about the pilots who flew the Spitfire fighter planes in the Battle of
Britain. Beside the book is a tie, embroidered with small Tudor roses and
a map of the British Isles, which was worn only by these pilots. Pages of
the book are turned daily, but relatives who wish to see a particular entry
can have the book taken out of its case for inspection.

Paul Nash 1889–1946
One of the official war artists during the first world war, who had
served at the front before being appointed. He painted in the same
capacity during the second world war. ' The Menin Road ' reflects his
experiences interpreted through his poetic imagination. His sense of
colour, the atmosphere of loneliness and fear, the few tiny figures in a
massive landscape, the shattered rocket shapes, trees, turbulent smoke-
filled skies ablaze with searchlights and the still, icy water convey the
horror of a country at war.

Stanley Spencer 1891–1959
One of the most original of this century's painters. He had a kind of
naïve religious feeling which he translated into his own style (as did
William Blake in his time). Spencer was in the RAMC in Macedonia
during the first world war. Later he painted an altarpiece, ' Resurrection ' of the Soldiers ', a huge ' Resurrection ' and ' Christ Carrying the
Cross ' which were set in Cookham, his home village. These can be seen
in the Tate Gallery. The hundred or so sketches he made of shipbuilding
of the Clyde during the second world war are in the museum.

Women's services
There is a collection of uniforms from the second world war, including those worn by the Women's Royal Naval Service, the Auxiliary
Territorial Service and the Women's Auxiliary Air Force. The work
carried out by these services is described and further information about
their wartime experiences can be found in a number of books available
from public libraries. One of the first was written by a Wren, Edith
Pargiter; its title is *She Goes to War*. Today the ATS and the WAAF
are known as the Women's Royal Army Corps and the Women's Royal
Air Force.

Ideas for classwork based on visits to the Imperial War Museum
1   Using ideas from museum exhibits, write about or paint your own
impressions of a battle with planes, soldiers in tanks or on foot and guns
in (a) the desert, (b) an airfield, (c) the jungle.
2   Study one of the models of street battles in France in the second

world war and find the uniforms of the soldiers involved. Write a story about the battle as seen through the eyes of a French housewife and illustrate part of it.

3 Paint a picture showing one of the jobs performed by the British during the second world war. Study the pictures in the art gallery for ideas and details of clothes and trades.

4 Study the planes in the museum, make a sketch of one and use it to paint a picture entitled 'The Deserted Airfield'. Try to convey a feeling of mystery and neglect with the plane (or part of it) looming up like a macabre monster.

5 Write a poem describing an aircraft carrier and an incident connected with it.

6 Find a cruiser, a submarine, a destroyer, an air-sea rescue boat, a frigate and a mine sweeper. Sketch one of them; then imagine that you are (a) the captain, (b) a rating or (c) the cook and paint a picture of some aspect of your day's work.

7 Make a model of a gun on its carriage or a tank, using balsa wood, cardboard cylinders and any other suitable materials.

8 Study camouflage, weapons and uniforms and paint or model a scene from jungle warfare, incorporating animals and plants if you like. Try to reflect the emotions of the soldiers involved. Write an account of the fighting as witnessed by a reporter.

9 Make a poster advertising the Imperial War Museum, using appropriate lettering.

10 Make a booklet with illustrations and short descriptions of each of the following: (a) a medal, (b) a fighter plane, (c) a member of the forces, (d) a ship in action. Design a suitable cover.

11 Write a story comparing the life of a sailor in the last war with one in Nelson's time. Draw both sailors, each in his correct uniform and against an appropriate background.

12 Design a medal or ribbon awarded to a member of the forces or a civilian for an act of bravery during the second world war. The design should show clearly why the medal is being awarded.

13 Write about and illustrate changes which took place between the first and second world wars in the design of the following: (a) a major's uniform, (b) a plane, (c) a gun, (d) a nurse's uniform.

14 Decide which of the services you would most like to join and write about the reasons for your choice. Draw the uniform, describe and illustrate the kind of work you would like to do and state in which foreign country you would like to be stationed.

15 Imagine that during the first world war you were a soldier in the Royal Horse Artillery and fired the British Army's first round in France from the 13-pounder gun. Write about this experience, with illustrations.

16 Imagine that you were a sailor in the first world war on board HMS

Lance, and fired the Royal Navy's opening shot in the war at sea. Write about this action, with illustrations.

17   In both world wars official artists were appointed to depict battles, the various types of work that went on and their own impressions of memorable events. Choose two paintings from each war. Describe them, discuss the style of painting and state who the artists were.

18   Find out all you can about one of the following, from models, equipment and displays: (a) the Gallipoli landings, 1915, (b) the Battle of Keren, 1941, (c) the Battle of Cassino, 1944. Write an essay or a poem about the event you have studied.

19   While Rupert Brooke was in the forces during the first world war he wrote a poem, ' The Soldier ', containing these lines: ' If I should die, think only this of me: That there's some corner of a foreign field that is forever England.' Find out all you can about Brooke and read some of his other poems. (There is a portrait of him in the National Portrait Gallery.)

20   Having looked at planes, tanks and ships from the second world war ask at your public library for books written by or about war heroes who served in the forces. One of the most moving and inspiring is *The Last Enemy* by Richard Hillary, about his life in the Royal Air Force. He died soon after the book was published. Imagine that you were one of these men or women and write a poem or some prose about your hopes, fears and doubts at the time.

LIVERPOOL CITY MUSEUM   William Brown Street, Liverpool

Antiquities. Enamels. Jewellery. Maritime material. Masks. Geological, botanical and zoological material. Aquarium. Planetarium.

Δ   *Apply to Museum Education Officer*.   Saturday morning club. Holiday activities.

Some exhibits in the Liverpool City Museum

Kingston brooch
A large gold circular Anglo-Saxon brooch 1 m (3 ft 3 in) across. The design consists of flat pieces of red garnet and blue lapis lazuli set in small cells.

Brass equatorium
Made in 1610, to find the geocentric positions of planets, moon and sun.

Porcelain punch pot
Eighteenth-century pot decorated in underglaze blue from Seth Pennington's Pottery, Liverpool. There are figures and landscapes on the lid and round the middle of the pot.

Slave carrying a lotus jar (Egyptian) 1400–1350 BC
Figure with skirt, bending under the weight of an enormous jar. Note the
placing of the head, legs, shoulders and arm, emphasising the load. Decorative textures on the jar and skirt.

History of Liverpool
New gallery illustrating the social, industrial and commercial background
of the port.

Model of mammoth
Pleistocene diorama. Compare this long-haired monster with our present-
day elephant.

Ideas for classwork based on visits to the Liverpool City Museum
1   Study the African masks and design one of your own in a collage
made with string, coloured papers, fabrics or dried materials such as peas
and spaghetti.
2   Choose a vehicle in the transport section, and imagine you are in
charge of it. Make up a story about it (a day's journey, for example),
describing the vehicle, the people in it (their costumes and personalities)
and the landscape and buildings you pass. Illustrate.
3   Make a booklet with writing and pictures illustrating four aspects of
the history of shipping.
4   How many musical instruments in the museum have flowers or
animals painted on them? Which have the most beautiful shapes?
5   You are a photographer. Choose three exhibits which are unusual,
interesting in shape, differently textured and would make exciting pictures, from one of the following sections: (a) zoology, (b) botany, (c)
geology, (d) archaeology. Describe them and say how you would photograph them. What background would you use? Would the *whole* object
be included, or just a part of it? Would lighting be subdued or strong?
6   Make a group mural with eight animals which represent eight different countries. Look for these in the museum and carry out the designs
in batik.
7   Imagine you are one of the following: (a) a bird, (b) a monkey,
(c) a fish. Paint a picture or cartoon of how visitors look to you as
they gaze into your aviary, cage or aquarium. Use models from the
museum.
8   Imagine you are appearing in a new discussion programme on television called ' Teenage Topics '. The theme is ' Museums ' and the following subjects are to be covered: (a) discovery, (b) humour, (c)
tragedy, (d) fear, (e) birth, (f) death, (g) invention. Find items which
relate to each of these and organise the programme among yourselves.
9   Choose an exhibit from one of the following groups to adapt for a

paper sculpture model: (a) clocks, (b) birds, animals and fish, (c) flowers, (d) faces.

10 Look round the gallery showing the history of Liverpool. Imagine you are going to work in one of the following capacities: (a) social, (b) industrial, (c) commercial. Describe what you would be doing and the building and street in which you would be working.

11 You are going to arrange an exhibition at the museum entitled 'Liverpool, Then and Now' which includes one typical exhibit from years ago and one from today from each of the following categories: (a) shipping, (b) entertainment, (c) art, (d) craft. What would you choose?

12 Draw an abstract design based on the brass equatonium made in 1610. Make a collage or embroidered picture with a selection of coloured strings or gold and silver cords and braids.

LONDON MUSEUM

Kensington Palace, The Broadwalk, Kensington Gardens, W8 New address will be in the Barbican.

History of London from earliest times. Stone Age finds. Roman collections: sandals, tombstones. Saxon weapons, silver and brass. Medieval bone skates, carved wooden church door frame, 'bird warble', hunting spear, dice and bone counters, finger-rings with magic inscriptions, German stoneware imports. Miniature street model, dioramas of Old St Paul's and the Great Fire of London. Stuart period: domestic utensils and implements. Georgian London: costume, enamels, watches, jewellery. Royal gifts and loans. State apartments. Toys. Theatre material. Pottery. Crafts. Furniture. Painting.

Δ *Apply to Schools' Service Officer.* Quiz sheets for children. Holiday programmes.

Some exhibits in the London Museum
Roman collections
In AD 43 the Romans under Claudius invaded Britain, remaining until about AD 410. Their building projects in London included a fort, a palace, a wooden bridge, a market place and public baths. Roman remains have been found in the mud at the bottom of the Thames and dug up during excavations for new buildings. The museum has an altar-stone from the temple of Mithras, a jug found in Southwark, surgical instruments, gaming equipment, glass, leatherwork, complete leather sandals, tombstones and sculptures. Reconstructed views suggest the appearance of the Roman city at various stages in its development.

Sixteenth century exhibits
Models of St Paul's and London Bridge. Craftwork – evidence of London's growing prosperity in medieval days – including arms and armour, metal, pottery, heraldic badges and leather work.

Civil War
Relics of Charles I including the blue silk shirt and knitted vest worn on the day of his execution. A death-mask of Oliver Cromwell. Hanging flasks on a bandolier belonging to one of Cromwell's soldiers: each contained the correct amount of gunpowder for charging a musket.

Costumes
These range from about 1600 to the present day. There is the tiny close-fitting wedding dress worn by Queen Victoria, the one worn by Queen Mary and the little white lace dresses worn by the present Queen Elizabeth and Princess Margaret at their father's coronation in 1937.

Dolls
Queen Victoria's dolls which she dressed herself when she was a child living at Kensington Palace. They all have names and stand on a miniature staircase. Queen Mary's dolls' house, complete with dolls in costume having a picnic.

Model street
A busy scene at Piccadilly. Three Georgian shops: an ironmonger's, a milliner's and a stationer's. Figures include a cross old lady shaking her umbrella, a coal merchant with bags of coal, a rearing horse and its driver and a lamplighter, as well as miniature victorias and hansom cabs. The figures are about 25 mm (1 in.) high.

Stuart period
This is well represented by costume, needlework, pottery, glass, pewter, implements and domestic utensils. There is an outstanding collection of jewellery which may have belonged to a City merchant from Cheapside.

Ideas for classwork based on visits to the London Museum
1 Look carefully at all the exhibits that appeal to you most. Illustrate and write about the history of one of the following: (a) pictures, (b) costumes, (c) furniture, (d) transport, (e) weapons. An interesting book for the form could be compiled using the best account of each topic.
2 Look for information about early man in the Thames Valley. Make notes on conditions, weapons, tools, food, clothes and the kind of society that existed at the time. Write an account of life then as if you were one of those early men, and illustrate it with three pictures.

3 Imagine you were an onlooker at the execution of Charles I. Write some prose or a poem about it and paint a picture of the event.

4 Illustrate three of the following, commenting on the materials involved: (a) the uniform of a Cromwellian soldier, (b) Queen Victoria's wedding dress, (c) Queen Victoria's coronation robe, (d) the robe and petticoat of pale yellow silk with embroidered stomacher, 1720–30, (e) a costume worn by an actor or ballet dancer.

5 Look at the State Apartments, especially the bedroom occupied by Princess Victoria before she became queen. Imagine you are the young princess, aged nine, and describe a morning in your life. You could talk about the view from from your window, favourite dresses, dolls, the pram you wheel about the garden and anything else you think a little princess living in the nineteenth century would think about and do.

6 Among the firearms is a flintlock blunderbuss which was used by a man who tried to assassinate William III when he was on his way home from hunting in Richmond. Find out more about this incident and write an account of what happened. What clothes were the king, his friends and the assassin wearing? How did the man approach the king, what did he say, who restrained him and how? What did Richmond Park look like in those days? The best stories might be illustrated or tape-recorded.

7 There is a fine gameboard with pieces that James II gave to Samuel Pepys. Write a short essay about the king and Pepys. What was the latter's profession? Give an example of his work. Draw and paint the costumes each would have worn. Why do you think the king gave Pepys this particular present?

MADAME TUSSAUD'S Baker Street, NW1

Approximately 450 wax figures.*

Kings and queens of England
Henry VIII and his six wives. Elizabeth I. Victoria. Elizabeth II and the royal family.

Tableaux
The murder of the princes in the tower. The execution of Mary, Queen of Scots. The Sleeping Beauty (based on a portrait of Madame du Barry).

* Madam Tussaud's wax works present famous people in three dimensions – their full face, profile and backs of heads can be studied, likewise their sizes, heights, and clothes of the period.

Chamber of horrors
Robespierre. Crippen. Burke and Hare, who murdered fifteen people in
the nineteenth century. Various torture instruments.

Heroes (live)
People in present-day news: Muhammad Ali, Twiggy, stage, film and TV
personalities.

Battle of Trafalgar
Recreation of the decks of Nelson's flagship *Victory*: taped music playing ' Hearts of Oak ', crew, guns and other equipment, with dramatic
lighting, smoke and the smell of gunpowder. Cannons fire, ships collide
and masts collapse.

London Planetarium (next door to museum)

Ideas for classwork based on visits to Madame Tussaud's
1   Write a script for a discussion on television between one of the following couples, and describe their clothes and appearance: (a) Elizabeth
I and John Lennon on music, (b) Queen Victoria and Twiggy on fashion
(contrasting the conventional approach of Victorian times with today's
freedom in design), (c) Henry VIII and David Frost on philosophy or
marriage, (d) yourself and one of the following: Elizabeth I; Mary,
Queen of Scots; Henry VIII.
2   Give an account of the Battle of Trafalgar after looking at the
tableau, imagining that you were one of the crew.
3   Study the figures on the orlop deck where Nelson lies dying. Find
out who they are and describe the scene through the eyes of the doctor,
Hardy or any other person in the reconstruction.
4   A wax model of Madame Tussaud herself welcomes you at the
entrance to the museum. Her portrait can be seen in the National Portrait Gallery. Compare the two media used to depict her and say which
you prefer. Find out about her life and write an essay on it, with illustrations.
5   Which is your favourite section of the museum. Describe the exhibits
it contains and draw four of them.
6   Who is your favourite monarch? Find out about the main events in
his or her life and when they took place. Draw four articles of clothing
he or she is wearing.
7   Which is your favourite period of history? Discuss its architecture
and furniture, and describe two famous people who were alive at the
time. Illustrate your account with costume drawings.
8   Write a poem (it need not be in regular verse form) about one of the
murderers in the chamber of horrors. Make it dramatic, eerie, gloomy,

frightening or whatever else seems appropriate for the person concerned.

9 Choose one of the 'Historic Ministers' on view. What impression have you formed of his character? List some of his achievements during his ministry.

10 Which famous person who is not on view would you include in this exhibition. Describe him or her, the clothes to be worn, the position of the figure, any accessory you would include as a symbol and what you would write on the label.

NATIONAL GALLERY Trafalgar Square, WC2

Oil paintings. Schools and developments in painting. Works by Dutch, Flemish, German, Spanish, Italian (including Siennese, Florentine and Venetian), French (up to 1900) and British (Hogarth to Turner) painters. Artists include Giotto, Jan Van Eyck, Uccello, Raphael, Mantegna, Piero della Francesca, Leonardo da Vinci, Michelangelo, Titian, Goya, Rembrandt, El Greco, Rubens and Watteau.

Some exhibits in the National Gallery
Goya 1746–1828
Famous for his dynamic etchings, *Los Caprichos*, which are rich in fantasy and invention and technically superb. In his portraits he pounced on and recorded the most characteristic expression of his sitters – not always a popular move in the Spanish court. His paint quality has a wonderful feeling of lightness, freedom and spontaneity. The gallery possesses a superb portrait, 'Dona Isabel Cobos de Porcel', and a scene from *El Hechizado por Fuerza* which illustrates Goya's vein of fantasy.

Titian 1487–1576
The greatest of the Venetian painters. His method was to underpaint vigorously in Venetian red half-tones or white lead. Using red, black or yellow he would work up the light parts and create a figure with a few strokes. The picture was then left for months before he worked on it again. He used his fingers as well as brushes for painting, achieving a freedom of style, a very fine portrayal of form, richness of colour and tonal quality. In his disregard of contours in his later work it can be said that he almost anticipated impressionism. His picture *Bacchus and Ariadne* is a sensuous, glowing rendering of the pagan Renaissance, full of movement and rhythm. Bacchus leaps from a leopard-drawn chariot; fauns, satyrs and Bacchantes dance behind him. Ariadne forms a quiet contrast and, in her position on the canvas with her body and hand pointed towards the centre, balances the crowd on the right. Both sides merge to meet the central figure with the appropriately placed swirling

cloak. *Portrait of a Young Man* is worth studying for the wonderful painting of the blue sleeve, besides which it is superb portraiture.

Piero della Francesca 1410–1492 (see plate facing page 13)

Profound, timeless, classical, serene – there is a mathematical perfection in his forms and a feeling of tranquillity produced by his soft, pale colours. One of the most beautiful pictures by this Florentine artist in the gallery is *The Baptism of Christ*. The relationship in the placing of figures, hands, feet, the tree under which Christ is standing, the dove above his head, the figures behind the main characters and the landscape beyond has been studied by artists and sculptors throughout the ages. The meeting place of the folds of the drapery round Christ's body leads upwards to the angels on the left, and the folds of material on the central angel's left shoulder lead down to the winged angel's hand and back to the central shape – Christ. John the Baptist's left arm guides the eye to another figure bending over, which leads one back up past John's shoulder to his right arm holding the pan of water, attracting attention to the dove and also downwards to the body of Christ. The composition is framed by the leafy foliage embracing the figures: plants, trees, mountains, clouds, pieces of landscape and parts of figures all form linking and interesting verticals and horizontals. Not a single shape could be taken away from the picture without losing a vital part of the composition. Many artists and art students have used the picture to aid their understanding of these concepts by basing other subjects and ideas on the same architectural construction. Contour shapes left between the angels' drapery and feet, the ground and the tree are as interesting as the drapery, leg and tree-trunk shapes themselves. Correct colour choice also plays a great part in achieving interest, contrast and harmony.

Paolo Uccello 1397–1475

The Florentine painter (he also worked in mosaics and stained glass) who was obsessed with the search for perspective in art. He spent days and nights learning to foreshorten, to express distance and to portray large, small and smaller figures in his pictures. Horses and men in ' The Rout of San Romano' appear a little wooden, as he sought to make his figures so three-dimensional that they stood away from the background as though carved. The fallen warrior and the broken lances on the ground are placed so that they point towards the 'vanishing point' on the horizon. The correct choice of light and shade had not yet been mastered by Uccello so they could not be coupled here with his discoveries about perspective. The picture is gay and decorative (slightly reminiscent of Froissart's *Chronicles*), with a superb feeling for colour and a great sense of design.

Leonardo da Vinci 1452–1519
This artist was also a musician and a scientist who invented many applied scientific schemes such as flying machines. His attitude towards painting was frequently experimental, as he aimed passionately towards perfection in art, for instance using different colour variations in themes for ' The Virgin of the Rocks ' (one version can be seen in the gallery). Many of his drawings of animals, plants and figures reflect his constant search for scientific knowledge.

Georges Seurat 1859–91
Seurat made many preparatory studies for his carefully planned compositions. After experimenting with a variety of styles he became interested in the scientific theories of colour combination and colour perception. He began his famous ' pointillist ' technique by juxtaposing various sized spots of colour in a kind of mosaic style. If yellow was placed next to blue, for example, the seeing eye would merge these into green. The gallery has one of his most famous paintings, ' Une Baignade Asnières ', which was one of the first experiments in this direction.

Three schools of Italian painting
Siennese: a dream-like, somewhat ethereal quality; love of contour and beauty; sense of rhythm and richness; patronage by church and noblemen. Artists: Simone Martini, Duccio de Buoninsega, Stefano di Giovanni Sassetta.
Florentine: love of shape with colour added; patronage by church and noblemen. Artists: Giotto, Michelangelo, Leonardo da Vinci, Paolo Uccello.
Venetian: change from tempera to oil paint; love of oriental design and shape fused with colour; in mansions, palaces and great civic buildings; patronage by noblemen, merchants and civic officials. Artists: Veronese, Tiepolo, Tintoretto, Titian.

Primitive art
The expression ' primitive ' used in connection with art has three possible meanings.
1 Prehistoric and tribal art
The art of primitive man from (a) the Stone Age and (b) ancient Egypt, Babylon and Assyria; also contemporary art by natives of the South Sea Islands and parts of Asia, and the African negro. This kind of art is usually governed by certain rules and uses symbols to express ' fertility ', ' war ', ' death ', ' gods ' and other concepts. Egyptian art had to conform with directions issued by the priests, but the artist was allowed to portray, not only what he could see, but what he knew about his subject.

Etched half-armour. North Italian c 1560–80
Wallace Collection, London

Silver vase and cover, London hallmark 1805–6
Victoria and Albert Museum, London

2 Painters working before the sixteenth century particularly of the
Italian and Netherlandish schools
These include early Christian Byzantine artists from the fifth to the fifteenth centuries. Their work can be seen in the gallery and it will be
observed that they, too, were governed by religious requirements, which
consisted of special design, colour and pattern arrangements in two
dimensions, elongation of figures and certain decorative qualities which
enhanced the effect of remoteness and mysticism. Many aspects of
Giotto's work, such as his formalised shapes, link him strongly with this
kind of primitive art. Eric Newton wrote, in *European Painting and
Sculpture*: '. . . The Giotto–Cézanne period (say 1300–1900), those six
centuries mark the gradual solution of one problem after another in the
conquest of appearances. The solution of those problems had nothing
whatever to do with the greatness of the artists involved, nor with the
potency with which they communicated their message. It revolutionised
the artist's means but it brought him no nearer to his end. About 1276–
1387 Giotto, unaware of one half of the problems yet to be solved, is
still a giant, immeasurably more potent than the host of later artists
who could solve them with the greatest ease. What still matters is the
intensity of the artist's vision, not its scope.'

3 Sunday painters
Artists without formal training, often with the time to work only in their
off-duty hours, are regarded as possessing the 'innocent eye' of the
primitive. Early nineteenth-century American primitives were farm
workers who moved from place to place, taking as their subjects 'harvest
time' or 'funerals' or 'passing trains'. Henri Rousseau (1844–1910), a
customs official, was the first and best known of the Sunday painters (as
they were called at the time) allowed to exhibit their work among the
mixed styles in the Salon des Independants in 1886. He is well known
for his beautiful paintings of animals. The gallery has one of his famous
'Tiger' pictures.

The twentieth century will be remembered, no doubt, chiefly for its
atmosphere of stress, noise and excessive speed which is bound up with
technological advance. To a certain extent the choice of uncluttered,
simple lines for fashion, furniture, utensils and architecture is an attempt
to compensate for this. Likewise there is a strong attraction towards the
apparent simplicity and spontaneity of past and present primitive art.*

* The Chinese Liaou Tao-Chouen in the Dynasty of Songs said 'Look
for *talent* in clumsiness' meaning that all art should be 'searching' and
contain a 'reflected struggle' (and conveying that the 'slick' is 'non-
art'). Primitives do just this and the best of them contain originality, a
certain rhythm and unity, poetry and humility, and are often very moving to look at.

D

Ideas for classwork based on visits to the National Gallery

1   Rembrandt (1606–69) is considered by many people to have been the greatest artist of all time. Look at some of his pictures in the gallery, especially *Portrait of the Painter in Old Age* (one of sixty self-portraits), *Margaretha Trip* and *The Woman Taken in Adultery*. Why do you think people feel so deeply about this artist? What do you notice about his composition and use of colour, light and shade? Describe your favourite among his pictures.

2   Look at the unfinished picture *Combing the Hair* by Degas 1834–1917). Make notes about the following: (a) colour, (b) drawing, (c) movement, (d) anything else you have learnt about his work by looking at his other pictures. Read all you can about this artist and compare your ideas about him and his work with what you have found in books. If you disagree with the books say why.

3   Look at *The Virgin and Child with Saints* by Duccio (active 1278, died 1319). Describe the picture in terms of colour and design and say whether it appeals to you.

4   Read the biblical description of 'The Agony in the Garden' and then compare and contrast the two portrayals of this subject by Mantegna (c 1431–1506) and Giorgione Bellini (c 1459–1516). Which rendering do you prefer? Does either resemble what was in your mind while reading the Bible story?

5   What do you think of the treatment and composition of *The Whim of the Young Saint Francis to Become a Soldier* by the Siennese artist Sasseta (c 1400–50)?

6   Look at the paintings by Michelangelo in the gallery and consult books illustrating his sculpture. Which medium do you prefer as regards his work? Give a short account of his life, mentioning the main events, and describe his character.

7   Hubert and Jan Van Eyck are often credited with the invention of oil-paint; they were certainly among the first to use it. Look for the painting by Jan Van Eyck entitled 'The Betrothal of the Arnolfini', for which he used oil instead of egg to bind the powder colours together. What advantage did this have over materials used previously?

8   Look at 'The Courtyard of a House in Delft' by Pieter de Hoogh (1629–84 or later). What strikes you about the mood of the picture, the colour and the light?

9   The painting by Vermeer (1632–75) called *A Young Woman Standing at a Virginal* is on view in the gallery. How does this compare and contrast with the painting by Pieter de Hoogh? Which do you prefer and why?

10   Make a list of titles of paintings in the gallery. Use one as the title for an original picture of your own.

11   Pick your favourite portrait from among the following, and state the reasons for your choice:
(a) *Portrait of Susanna Lunden* by Rubens (1577–1640), (b) *The Shrimp Girl* by Hogarth (1697–1764), (c) *Dr Peral* by Goya (1746–1828), (d) *Madame Moitessier* by Ingres (1780–1867).

12   Look at the picture *The Annunciation with S Emidius* by Crivelli (1457–93). Write down a list of the patterning you can see in it (for example, peacock's tail).

NATIONAL MARITIME MUSEUM
Romney Road, Greenwich, SE10

A ship's bell opposite the door in the west wing sounds the watches. Navigation instruments, uniforms, arms and relics. Famous sea captains: Sir Francis Drake and Lord Nelson (bloodstained uniform from Trafalgar and relics). Captain Cook gallery. Whaling and polar exploration. Astrolabes, globes and clocks. Special gallery for temporary exhibitions. Paintings, drawings and prints: artists include Turner, Lely, Brooking, Reynolds, Chambers, Hilliard, Hogarth, Romney, Van de Veldes (father and son) Whistler, and Gainsborough. Queen's house: Palladian architecture by Inigo Jones, completed in 1635 for the wife of Charles I, Queen Henrietta Maria; former studio (next to orangery) of the Van de Veldes (father and son); beautiful Great Hall with black and white marble sun design floor; staircase with decorative iron balustrade known as the ' tulip ' design. New Neptune Hall: the original *Reliant* paddle-tug, the *Dunola*, a Thames conservancy launch, two State barges, sail loft, boat shop, history of the boat with originals on display, figureheads and ship models. Coins and medals. Two world wars: merchant vessels and marine art. Lecture hall with closed circuit television. Films.
Δ   *Apply to Education Officer.*   Children's art and craft studio and boat building facilities in education centre. Holiday programme.

Old Royal Observatory (complex)   Greenwich Park, Greenwich, SE10
Flamsteed House
Designed by Sir Christopher Wren. Sandglasses and sundials. Navigation instruments.

Meridian building
Astronomical instruments, many in their original settings. The Greenwich Meridian Line in the courtyard.

South London Planetarium
Demonstrations given.

Some exhibits in the National Maritime Museum

Patchboxes and snuffboxes
Over seventy decorative Staffordshire enamel boxes, used for face 'patches', jewellery, or snuff. These popular trinkets were produced in the late eighteenth and early nineteenth centuries to commemorate the Battle of Trafalgar and the death of Nelson.

Memorial ring
Worn by Thomas Bolton, later the second Earl Nelson, at Nelson's funeral. Lost the day afterwards and found by a gardener forty years later.

Circular paintings on glass
Made to commemorate the victory at the Battle of the Nile, 1 August 1798. They show Nelson's flagship *Vanguard* and the *Culloden*.

Celestial globe by van Langeran (Amsterdam)
Made in 1625 by painting in oils on paper stuck to plaster. Beautifully coloured stars with paintings of a swan, dragon, queen, bull, soldier, scorpion, lion, raven, crab and serpent to illustrate the constellations.

Paddle-tug
Paddle-steamers have been a familiar sight in British ports, harbours and coastal water for 150 years. This method has been used to propel ferries, tugs, ocean liners, trawlers and warships. In the Neptune Hall is a reconstruction of the twentieth-century paddle-tug *Reliant* with working engines and paddle-wheel. Visitors can explore the engine room and walk about on deck.

Battle of Solebay 1672 (tapestry)
Woven from a design by William Van de Velde. Tapestries were used to decorate walls, exclude draughts and keep rooms warm. Many hands must have been needed to complete this work.

Crow's nest
A platform for the look-out man from HMS *Discovery*, used on the Arctic expedition in 1875–6. Model of look-out man included. ('There's a sweet little cherub that sits up aloft and looks out for the life of poor Jack.')

Figureheads
These have an affinity with early Greek statues, which were painted and had jewels attached to the eyes and clothing for a richer and more magnificent effect. Figureheads were made partly for decorative pur-

poses and partly as a defence against evil spirits and bad luck. Some popular models for figureheads were the Virgin Mary, Britannia, kings and queens, pagan gods (especially Neptune).

Sailor's crafts
Painting and drawing depends in the first instance on seeing, either inwardly or outwardly. Sailors who were trained to ' look out ' at sea had plenty of time for this in their off-duty hours. From the late eighteenth century onwards their chief pursuits were recording details of voyages and ships, by writing, drawing, painting or sewing, decorating scrimshaw, making ships in bottles or fashioning belts and plaited craftwork, for all of which materials were always available. The results were either kept for reference, or sold ashore, or perhaps given to their families. In the days before photography there were many untrained artists who could keep records of voyages and portray sea battles, ships and crews, lands they visited and details of landfalls for identification as an aid to navigation.

Ideas for classwork based on visits to the National Maritime Museum
1   Compare an admiral's uniform in Nelson's day with the one worn now.
2   Study the design on the commemorative patchboxes and snuffboxes and make clay ' pinch pots ' with a nautical design on the lid.
3   Make a booklet about Captain Cook's voyages, mentioning the following: (a) animals seen on the voyage, (b) favourite flowers, (c) food, (d) navigation instruments, (e) native costume.
4   Design a ship's flag to paint or print in batik.
5   Paint a picture of one of the following artists sketching on a beach or quayside or in a harbour: Turner, Van de Velde (father or son), Brooking, Chambers, Wyllie. The works of each should tell you where you would have been most likely to find him.
6   Study some of the macramé in the museum and make an abstract design based on a navigation instrument using this medium. A wire frame may help. Use different thicknesses of string.
7   Make a group painting of a sea subject. Use the Chinese technique where one person paints hands, another faces, another boats, and so on.
8   Design in wood some small decorated spears for hunting in the Arctic; paint them.
9   Paint or model a typical Arctic scene.
10   Paint a picture of one of the following: (a) two sailors fighting on board ship, (b) a fire on board ship during a battle, (c) a ship sinking during a battle at sunset.
11   Make a model of a ship from (a) straws, paper, boxes, tubes, etc, or (b) balsa wood, cotton, etc.
12   Use plaster, polystyrene, wire and other materials to construct a

group structure large enough to walk into, based on the shapes of the museum's moving timekeepers, compasses, sextants, bronze gilt globes and brass spheres.

13 Make a globe from pieces of paper stuck on to a blown-up balloon and decorate it with pictures of mermaids, animals fish and other things associated with land or sea.

14 Among the figureheads in the Neptune Hall at the museum are a gannet and a lion made from sections of carved wood. Study these and carve a miniature version of one of them, or model it in papier mâché.

15 Illustrate *Moby Dick* as dramatically as you can in a four-frame strip cartoon.

16 Paint or model a boat with your own whaling symbols on it.

17 Make a medal from papier mâché, cardboard or thin copper. Decorate with paint or coloured paper; or by etching into the copper.

18 Make decorative swords from sticks and cut cardboard cylinders, wound round with paper, silver foil, wool and ribbon.

19 Make a piece of abstract sculpture based on a breastplate.

20 Search on a seashore or by a river for the kind of objects that are often washed ashore from wrecks, for example pipes, tea chests, bottles and brooches.

20 Write a short history of either Lord Nelson or Sir Francis Drake, dealing with his birthplace and boyhood, the ships he sailed in, battles won and lost, personal relics and the period in which he lived. Illustrate the text with postcards, reproductions, drawings and paintings.

21 Write a short history of one aspect of passenger travel at sea, covering (a) early travel – mail boats, immigration (discomfort and conditions), food, scurvy, 'Malta dog' and (b) present-day travel – P & O, Royal Mail steamers, cargo ships. Illustrate.

22 Choose a figurehead and write about its appearance and colour, where it travelled, the type of ship it belonged to and any superstition connected with it. Illustrate.

23 Write about a recent discovery of a ship, for example the Graveney boat found in Kent in October 1970. Describe how it was removed, pieced together and treated to prevent decay. Illustrate.

24 Study a thread picture made by a sailor. Make a fabric collage, batik or embroidered picture based on a sailing design. Simplify the sails and rigging but try to copy the outlines accurately. Fill in a suitable background.

25 A deep sea diver is inspecting a shipwreck at the bottom of the ocean. Look round the museum for the kind of things he might find, such as cannons, arms, pottery and jewellery. Use them as models for a picture.

26 Paint a picture or make a fabric collage or model of Flamsteed House surrounded by trees in winter or spring.

27 Collect all the information you can about the working conditions

and discoveries of the first Astronomer Royal at Flamsteed House, and compare them with those of a present-day astronomer. Make a booklet about your findings, setting out the old methods and ideas on left-hand pages and their modern equivalents on the right. Illustrate wherever possible.

28 Decide which room you like best in Flamsteed House. Imagine you are a king, queen, astronomer, navigator or artist living in the seventeenth, eighteenth or nineteenth century and describe an hour of your life spent in the room. Illustrate.

29 Look at the ceremonial pictures depicting funerals, weddings, siege celebrations, coronations and royal visits.

(a) Paint your own ship ceremonial occasion. It can be: Primitive (native fishing boats bringing in the fish). Egyptian (with funeral pyres). English (commemerating Queen Victoria's coronation – with flags and fireworks, Sir Francis Chichester's return in *Gipsy Moth*).

30 Make a toy theatre and design secenery and figures for a play based on the life and death of Nelson.

31 Look at the papercut made *c* 1800 of events from a naval officer's life. Make your own papercut picture, using scissors, a Stanley knife or a razor blade with a protective handle, basing the design on an event in the life of Captain Cook, Lady Hamilton or any other famous person connected with the museum.

32 After looking at paintings of the sea and models of ships in the museum, go back to school and listen to *Peter Grimes* by Benjamin Britten. The music conveys the atmosphere of stormy seas and the emotions that go with them. Paint a fishing boat tossing admidst high, fierce waves, grey skies and clouds, wind and salt spray.

NATIONAL PORTRAIT GALLERY
St Martin's Place, Trafalgar Square, WC2

Five thousand authentic portraits, including drawings, paintings, miniatures, statues, engravings and photographs, of men and women in British history from the Tudors up to the present day. Among them are (a) *Elizabeth I* by the younger Gheeraerts, (b) *George VI and his family* by Gunn, (c) *Henry VIII* by Holbein, (d) *Lady Hamilton* by Romney, (e) *Sir Walter Raleigh* by Hilliard, (f) *Sir Winston Churchill* by Sickert, (g) *Self portrait* by Gainsborough, (h) *Thomas Howard, Earl of Arundel* by Rubens, (i) *Warren Hastings* by Reynolds. Each room has or will be given a historical theme, and portraits will be supplemented by furniture, swords, prints and drawings. Marble, bronze and stone are some of the materials used for statues, statuettes, busts, medals and coins.

Δ *Apply to Education Officer*. Holiday competitions. Opportunities for children's creative participation: An example was portrait photographs which were taken by the children with polaroid cameras in a studio set up for the purpose, complete with lighting, props and dressing-up clothes; advice and instruction was given by photographic experts.

Some exhibits in the National Portrait Gallery

In the gallery there are pictures by many different artists, some famous, some virtually unknown; but every portrait on view is accepted as authentic in likeness and costume and illustrates part of a period in history. Portraits can take a number of different forms:

(a) a faithful reproduction of features requiring little artistry
(b) a heightening or distortion of certain features (caricature)
(c) a silhouette, painted or made from black paper
(d) a photograph or film
(e) a likeness which is also a work of art.

Clothes can tell a great deal about the period the sitter lived in. In the seventeenth century, for example, it was fashionable for people to be painted dressed up as ancient Romans or shepherdesses. Kings and queens are usually portrayed in the full paraphernalia of crowns, robes and orbs, scientists with their scientific instruments, famous seamen with their ships or anchors, and so on.

Styles in portraiture vary according to the fashion of the day, the preference of the sitter or the taste of the artist. In the sixteenth century people were treated as symbols of rank and power, their individual characteristics being largely ignored as unimportant; in the seventeenth, an informal fashionable idealism was the dearest wish of the sitters; in the eighteenth the family group, in or out of doors, became popular, and Reynolds often painted his sitters in the classical poses of which he was so fond.

The following portraits come to mind as works of art in portraiture, in different styles and at different periods. The first can be seen in the National Portrait Gallery and the others are in the National Gallery.

Thomas Howard. Earl of Arundel by Rubens
Dona Isabel Cobos de Porcel by Goya
Portrait of Saskia in Arcadian Costume by Rembrandt
Portrait of a Young Man by Titian.

Portrait painters find interest in the play of light and shade in features, hair and skin, and in the shape of mouth, eye, shoulder, nose, neck and hand in relation to each other and to the background, which can be abstract or realistic and often reflects the sitter's interests. The aim of all good portrait painters is to attain a deep appreciation of their sitter's personality, coupled with an imaginative likeness, and all the infinite values which go towards good design; and if they do not already know them well they may spend some hours with them before they begin to paint, talking to them and getting to know their attitudes, interests, likes and dislikes, so that they can paint, in their own particular style, as true a picture as possible.

Silhouette portraits
There is a good example of a silhouette picture (made in 1832) by Auguste Edouart, one of the best known and finest paper collage cutters, of ' Four Actors in Glasgow ', a portrait of Alexander, Weekes, Thurdon and Lloyd. Silhouette paintings date from the Ice-age in the Agua Amarga caves in Spain (figures in flight). Early Egyptian and Greek vases had decorative silhouetted motifs (people and animals). It is believed that this form of profile portraiture arose from attempts to trace the outline of the shadows of people and objects. Later, pictures were painted or cut from black paper and projection equipment was used to reduce or enlarge the shadow cast. The invention of photography was a great aid. Cardboard, glass, ivory, wax and plaster were also used in the eighteenth and early nineteenth century. Modern advertising makes use of the silhouette.

Self-portrait by Hogarth (1697–1764)
This picture, painted towards the end of Hogarth's life, portrays him in informal dress and without a wig. He has just drawn the Muse of Comedy on his canvas. Hogarth was famous for his morality series: *The Harlot's Progress, The Rake's Progress* and *Marriage a la Mode. The Shrimp Girl*, one of his best spontaneous portraits, can be seen in the National Gallery.

Thomas Howard, Earl of Arundel by Rubens (1577–1640)
The Earl of Arundel was dedicated to the revival of the arts in England; he possessed a vast collection of renaissance paintings and classical antiquities. Rubens painted this great portrait (which is a first sketch) during a visit to England. A three-dimensional approach (in contrast with the two dimensional style of the previous century), rich texture and superb and dramatic lighting effects characterise his baroque style of art.

Henry VIII by Hans Holbein the Younger (1497–1543)
This portrait is known as *The Chatsworth Cartoon* and was the original drawing for a wall-painting in Whitehall Palace, destroyed by fire in 1697. The cartoon is assembled, like a collage, from cut-outs mounted on a large sheet of paper. Hundreds of pinpricks which follow the main lines of the composition enabled the artist to transfer the drawing on to the wall. The painting celebrated the king's achievements by illustrating his greatest triumphs.

The Brontë Sisters by Patrick Branwell Brontë c 1835
This portrait of Anne, Charlotte and Emily Brontë, novelists and poets,
has a space in the centre where it is thought that their brother originally
painted a picture of himself which he subsequently blanked out. The
marks across the top of the picture were made when Charlotte's husband
folded it up and left it on top of a cupboard.

T S Eliot by Patrick Heron
An abstract impression showing the front and side views merged into one.
It is interesting to compare this with the portrait of Eliot sculpted by
Epstein.

Ideas for classwork based on visits to the National Portrait Gallery
1   Choose a poet, musician or adventurer whose portrait hangs in the
gallery. Describe the picture and write a short essay about the life and
achievements of the subject.
2   Much can be learnt in the gallery about costume, furniture and social
history. Name one portrait which conveys information of this kind, describe it and draw the most interesting items of dress or furniture, or
whatever you think is significant among the other objects included.
3   Study drawings, paintings, miniatures, sculpture and original costumes
and make an illustrated list of seven styles in collar design from different periods.
4   What would you expect to be the main differences between a portrait
painted by a great artist and one recorded by the camera of a great
photographer. Which method of portraiture do you prefer and why?
5   Choose three interesting portraits of people from one of the following
groups: (a) kings and queens, (b) poets, (c) statesmen, (d) inventors,
(e) explorers. Write an essay explaining why the pictures interest you,
how they differ in the treatment of their subjects and what they tell you
about the sitters.
6   Compare any portrait of Elizabeth I with any portrait of Elizabeth
II by discussing costumes, accessories, reflection of the social life of their
respective periods, the style of portraying royalty and the methods of
painting and creating likenesses.
7   Find and describe portraits which illustrate the following items: (a)
three different types of wig, (b) three different types of shoe, (c) three
different types of coat.
8   Look at a self-portrait by one of the following: (a) Dante Gabriel
Rossetti, (b) Sir Jacob Epstein, (c) Thomas Gainsborough, (d) Sir
Godfrey Kneller. What do you think it reveals about the artist? Write
a brief description of his life and times and describe one of his paintings
of sculptures that you like.
9   Paint or draw a portrait of a member of your family, a friend or

anyone with well-marked features. Study the proportions of the face which are, very roughly: eyes halfway between top of head and chin, tip of nose halfway between eyes and chin, mouth a third of the distance between tip of nose and chin. Are the eyes large, small, prominent, deep-set, round or slit? Eyebrows arched or straight? Nose long or short, wide or narrow, snub or pointed? Mouth thin, full, smiling, thoughtful, bad-tempered? Chin prominent or receding? Hair straight or curly, fine or thick? Ears large or small, flat or protruding? Concentrate on achieving as good a likeness as possible.

10 Look for the following portraits: (a) Rupert Brooke, 1887–1915, pencil drawing (posthumous) by J H Thomas, (b) Lord Byron, 1788–1824, by Richard Westall, (c) John Keats, 1795–1821, miniature by J Severn. Write a short account of each poet's life, comment on what the portrait reveals of his character and quote your favourite poem by each. If a film was being made about the lives of these three men to which actors would you give their parts?

11 Choose (a) a television star, (b) an author, (c) one of your neighbours. Describe him or her and say what symbolic objects you would include in full-length photograph.

12 Look at some of the caricatures in the gallery; note how some have enlarged heads and feature, exaggerated figures or unnatural appendages such as wings. Comment on three of them, naming subject and artist. Try to draw someone you know using this style of portraiture.

13 Explain the symbols used in the engraving of Sir Francis Drake attributed to J Hondius (1583).

14 Look at the anonymous engraving of Guy Fawkes and the Gunpowder Plot conspirators. Use the face and costume of one of these men as the basis for a painting or linocut, and include a significant symbol.

15 Choose your favourite portrait from these three: (a) *Lytton Strachey* by H Lamb, (b) *Sir Arthur Sullivan* by J E Millais, (c) *Sir Winston Churchill* by W Sickert. Explain why you like it and give a short account of the lives of both artist and sitter.

16 Choose one of the portraits of children and write a story about a day in his or her life (set in the appropriate period).

17 Find a portrait drawing you do not like. Say what you dislike about it and suggest how it might have been improved.

18 Choose any period in history and find portraits of four people living at the time. Sketch their costumes and say which details of design are most typical of the period.

19 Find the following postcards: (a) Lady Jane Grey by 'Master John', (b) Elizabeth I by an unknown artist, (c) Sir Walter Raleigh by Nicholas Hilliard. Use one as the basis for a design for a wall-hanging in fabrics or a paper collage. The original portrait will help you with ideas

for colours and textures. Decorate with lace, sequins, glass beads, pearls, braids and ribbons.

20   Pick one of the following portraits from the museum collection and write a short biography of the sitter and the artist:

Lord Kitchener by Sir Hubert Herkomer, Charles James Fox by Karl Hickel, Isambard Brunel by John Horsley, Sir Edward Burne-Jones by Philip Burne-Jones, Sir George Darwin by Mark Gertler, Charles Lamb by William Hazlitt, Nell Gwynn by Sir Peter Lely, Warren Hastings by Sir Thomas Lawrence, Hannah More by Henry Pickersgill.

21   Imagine you are setting up your own portrait gallery. Think of one person (past or present) in the following categories and match up the medium best suited to that particular face. Give your reasons for your choice and aim to build up an interesting collection.

(a) King or Queen, (b) film star or television personality, (c) writer, (d) musician, (e) artist, (f) inventor or discoverer, (g) famous child, (h) famous politician, soldier, sailor or airman.

Media
(a) oil paint, (b) watercolour, (c) drawing, (d) linocut, (e) silhouette, (f) collage, (g) sculpture, (h) photograph.
Do a portrait in one of these media.

NATURAL HISTORY MUSEUM (BRITISH MUSEUM)
Cromwell Road, South Kensington, SW7

Fish and fish skeletons, starfish, corals, sponges, sea anemones, shells, giant blue whale (model). Elephants, tigers, lions, dinosaur gallery. Three animal dioramas in the Rowland Ward Pavilion. Human developments: eyes, skulls and bodies. Plants. Insects. Minerals. Birds from all countries, including the dodo, nests, eggs. Films.

Δ   *Apply to Teacher in Charge.*   Children's centre. Nature trails. Children aged 10–14 may join the Natural History Club after submitting an entrance project; Saturdays, except during August.

Some exhibits in the Natural History Museum
Mandrill
A grotesque animal with a red, blue and purple mask-like face and small yellowish pointed beard. The bald posterior is a brilliant reddish-violet. The fur is olive-brown mixed with grey. The ears are small, furless and coloured blue and black. Mandrills are found in Guinea.

Yak
The wild yak lives on high plateaux in central Tibet and other parts of Asia. It is sometimes called the ' grunting ox ' as it makes a sound like a

pig's grunt. The heavy fringes of hair on a yak's sides do not appear until the animal is three months old; the calves are covered in rough curling hair and have white bushy tails. These animals have a number of domestic uses: they provide milk and transport and their wool is used for making ropes.

Blue whale (model)
This model, about 27.7 m (91 ft) long was constructed according to measurements taken from whales caught in Antarctic waters. The blue whale is the largest creature ever known to live on this planet. Perhaps surprisingly, it lives on small shrimp-like creatures which it catches by sieving seawater through the blades of ' whalebone ' that grow downwards from its palate on each side of its mouth. Maritime museums often display objects made by sailors from this substance. The whale's body structure is only fitted for life in the water; if it is washed ashore by the waves it has no means of getting back to the sea and dies of hunger. In the whale hall there are photographs of early and modern methods of whaling, the purpose of which is to obtain the mammal's oil, meat and bones.

Parrot fish skeleton
The coral-eating fish to which this fossilised skeleton belonged was of a species that can grow to as much as 1.2 m (4 ft) in length. The solid yet delicate bones are fascinating to examine, resembling a jigsaw puzzle in which all the pieces fit together perfectly. Parrot fish are very striking in appearance, brilliantly coloured and interestingly patterned. The name of the fish may be derived from its colouring or from the strong teeth with which it crushes the corallines and which are curved like a parrot's beak.

Brittle star
The fossilised brittle star came from South Africa. These starfish are distinguished by their feathery arms. If touched they shatter into fragments, some of which grow into new starfish.

Ideas for classwork based on visits to the Natural History Museum
1 Sketch design for some monsters, suitable for use in a television play, based on some of the insects you have seen. The puss-moth caterpillar, the tiger beetle, the praying mantis and the longicorn beetle are among the most terrifying in appearance, especially when magnified. Suggest materials from which your monsters could be constructed.
2 Some jelly-fish have strange and exotic forms. Sketch one of the most interesting in the museum and paint a picture in which it almost fills the paper. Use blues, greens and greys for a background of seawater in the spaces left, and colour the jelly-fish with a mixture of gouache,

watercolour, pen and ink and coloured felt pens; scratch lines and patterns into the surface with a pin or an old pen nib, for added interest.

3 Make drawings of shells with spines and select one on which to base a machined fabric collage. Plain running stitch can look very attractive for outlines, like drawing with pen and ink; take the needle two or three times over the same area where you wish to achieve a darker effect. The following shells are ideal: (a) *Delphinula imperiatis*, South Pacific, (b) *Opisthostoma mirabile*, Sarawak, (c) *Murex purpuratus*, Indian Ocean.

4 Paint, or draw in pen and ink and colour with felt-tips, a picture entitled *The Gardens of the Sea*, with rocks, seaweeds, sea anemones and other underwater creatures. Try to reproduce the colours accurately.

5 Some British fungi have extraordinary shapes. Sketch and paint three of the following: (a) shining cup fungus, (b) magpie inkcap, (c) truffle, (d) fly agaric, (e) flower-headed thelephora, (f) birch-stump fungus. These could also be used in an abstract picture of textured tree trunk, or with animals and birds against a woodland background.

6 Some beetles resemble jewels in their colour and lustre. Look at some of the most attractive patterned ones, which include: (a) *Catoxantha bonvouloiri*, Assam and India, (b) *Chrysochroa edwardsi*, northern India, (c) *Acrocinus longimanus* (harlequin beetle), British Honduras, (d) *Sphingnotus mirabilis*, Solomon Islands, (e) *Euchroma gigantea*, British Guinea. Make a model of one of these, or of any other beetle you like, using painted papier mâché for the body and thin wires covered with strips of painted tissue paper for the legs.

7 Find a fossilised fish or the skull of an animal, such as a sheep, in the museum. Draw it carefully, observing how all the parts fit together. Now use this as the basis for a fabric collage or painting. If you decide to paint it, give it an appropriate setting, like a cave or a desert, or an outcrop of bare rock by the sea. The skeleton or skull should be the largest shape in the landscape, like a huge piece of sculpture.

8 Paint a picture entitled *Insects as seen by an Ant*; enormous fierce spiders, bees or wasps, beautiful giant butterflies and huge flowers, leaves and pebbles could be included.

9 Paint a group mural of the animals and birds you have sketched in the museum and a giant tree. This would be most effective on a piece of wall, using powder or acrylic paint.

10 Look out for photographs or drawings of objects seen through a microscope. For instance – the cells of a twig, or the sap avenues in an ivy stem, the stem of a flower like an arum lily, a real fir-cone cut crossways or sideways.

11 Look at these different shapes – claws and feet of burrowing animals (fox, fieldmouse and mole), claws and feet of birds (peewit, mallard and hoopoe) – draw them. They need a lot of study and will make subsequent

pictures of the whole bodies of birds or animals when standing or walking, more convincing. Discuss the variations with other members of the class.

SCIENCE MUSEUM (BRITISH MUSEUM)
Exhibition Road, South Kensington, SW7

Children's gallery: working scientific exhibits, illumination collections and models, domestic appliances, locks and fastenings, dioramas – transport by air, land and sea from prehistoric times to the present day, street and interior lighting, communications. Histories of power and land transport. Electric power development: models and dioramas, generation and distribution. Inventions: Parsons's steam turbine, Watt's steam engine, Trevithick's high-pressure engine and boiler. Transport: locomotives, horse-drawn vehicles, bicycles and motorcycles. Collection of hand and machine tools. Engineering. Textiles from raw materials. Iron and steel. Glass technology. Development of farming machinery: dioramas and scale models. Gas. Meteorology, time measurement, surveying and astronomy, mathematics and physics. Industrial and pure chemistry (including substances in everyday use). Sailing ships and small craft: models, some working. Aeronautics gallery. Space exploration. History of telecommunications: telegraph, telephone, radar and television equipment (including three ships' radio cabins with original equipment), first and second world war radio sets, models of communications satellites, Science Museum's demonstration radio station. Cinema.
Δ *Apply to Museum Lecturer.* Holiday activities.

Some exhibits in the Science Museum
The windmill
In fifteenth-century Holland, large stretches of farmland depended for their survival on the drainage windmills which the Dutch developed to help in their constant struggle to defend the land from the encroaching sea. With the spread of electricity during the last forty years they have become redundant, but hundreds of these decorative objects, still in working order, can be seen throughout Holland to this day. The windmills in Britain were nearly all flour mills. A model of the magnificent post mill formerly at Sprowston can be seen in the museum.

The phonograph
On Edison's earliest phonographs (1877) recording was done on a sheet of tinfoil wrapped round a cylinder. On later ones hard cylinders were used for pre-recorded material and wax ones for recording at home and in the office. The museum contains examples of these Edison machines and of those made by other firms such as Pathé. It also contains examples

of the earliest disc gramophones and of primitive instruments using magnetic recording, a technique that made the cylinder office phonograph obsolete, and is employed in the modern tape recorder.

The Rose engine

Accurate versions of the lathe, the fundamental machine tool, were first developed in connection with the making of watches and clocks. Rose engines were developed for ornamental turners and used to produce the regular patterns of decoration known as ' engine ' turning. Later versions were given attachments to make them more versatile to produce such items as chessmen and snuff boxes. The German engine of 1750 is itself an artistic object in rococo style.

Temple of Vesta

In the old Roman days Vestal Virgins maintained and guarded a flame in the Temple belonging to Vesta the goddess of the hearth. A chemical fire machine was made round about 1800 in the form of this Temple and in this miniature object hydrogen is generated and released through the mouth of a lion.

Ideas for classwork based on visits to the Science Museum

1 Make an abstract or interesting realistic picture of water in one of the following forms: (a) clouds, (b) dew on a spider's web, (c) a waterfall, (d) sea waves, (e) frost, (f) mountain mist.

2 Paint a picture of a miner working in the pit with his head-lamp and tools. This will be an exercise in the definition of areas of dark colours, lit only by the glow of the light. Pay careful attention to the textures of the coal and the appearance of the miner's mouth and eyes.

3 Make a poster in five colours advertising the museum (like the posters London Transport uses to persuade people to visit the countryside, stately homes, zoos, exhibitions and similar attractions). Include in the design: (a) a biplane, (b) a ship, with or without sails, (c) an old steam engine. It might be interesting to have the shapes overlapping in places: start by cutting them out of newspaper and juggling them around until they look intricate but not muddled. Keep the design simple – remember that the poster must be seen clearly from the other side of the road or the opposite platform. Use Letraset for the lettering if you like.

4 Trace the history of the sewing machine, listing the names of makers of each model and explaining how it was improved by each new invention.

5 Sketch one of the following model ships: (a) Egyptian ship c 1300 BC, (b) Greek war galley c 500 BC, (c) Roman merchant ship c AD 200, (d) Flemish carrick, c 1480. Use your drawing for a fabric or paper collage, incorporating thread, string, beads, lace and other decorative materials.

Detail of a page from The Codex Zouche-Nuttal. A Pre-Columbian Mixtec pictograph manuscript from Mexico, painted on deer skin
Museum of Mankind (Department of Ethnology)

opposite above Goat in white porcelain, modelled by Johann Joachim Kaendler for the Japanese Palace in Dresden, Meissen c 1732

opposite below Unglazed horse. T'ang Dynasty *Ashmolean Museum, Oxford*

above Onyx offering bowl in the form of an ocelot Teotihuacan culture, Mexico c AD 600 *The British Museum*

below Recumbent Figure 1938 by Henry Moore *The Tate Gallery, London*

Silver sauceboat with winged dragon handle. London *c* 1740
Ashmolean Museum, Oxford

6 Look at early examples of planes, trains, carriages and cars. Say which form of transport you think you would have preferred, name and date and describe one vehicle and say what you would have liked about it.

7 Choose one of the following boats: (a) Antung junk, (b) Norwegian herring boat, (c) tunny fishing boat. Describe a fishing expedition in it (including departure and return), as experienced by one of the crew.

8 Find a clock that interests you. Make a note of the type, the maker's name (if known) and the date it was made. Write a story about it using the following outline:

(1) It was sold in a shop, stolen or kept by the maker.

(2) It had three different owners at various times: a landowner, a composer and shipwright.

(3) It was dropped in a remote place and lost, thrown away or left in an attic.

(4) How did it come to be in the museum?

Make sure that any details of costume, architecture or furniture mentioned in the story are in period with the clock.

9 Look round the museum for something that could be adapted for a child's toy. Explain what materials you would use to make it, whether they would be safe and how long they would last. For which age range would it be most suitable. How could it develop a child's skill and observation?

TATE GALLERY Millbank, SW1

Paintings: (1) paintings from the Stuart period, (2) British paintings past and present, (3) modern foreign paintings. Artists include: Hogarth, Gainsborough, Reynolds, Turner (revolutionised English painting), Constable (changed the approach to painting nature), Blake (religious fantasy), Palmer (landscapes), Stubbs (horses), Manet and Monet (impressionists), Seurat (pointillist), Henri Rousseau (le Douanier, ' Sunday painter '), Whistler (landscapes and portraits), Millais (pre-Raphaelite), Cézanne (cubist – classical renaissance), Klee (free fantasy or ' taking a line for a walk '), Matisse (post-impressionist), Picasso (blue period, cubist, metamorphic phase, odalisques), Mondrian (abstraction – neoplasticism), Leger (cubism), Graham Sutherland, Stanley Spencer, Francis Bacon, Jackson Pollock, Ceri Richards, Bridget Riley. Examples of constructionism, abstract, expressionism, tachism, op, pop and kinetic art.

Sculpture: Henry Moore, Sir Jacob Epstein, Auguste Rodin, Elizabeth Frink, Bernard Meadows.

Δ *Apply to Education Officer.* Introductory talks for children by arrangement. Society for children: Young Friends of the Tate.

E

Some exhibits in the Tate Gallery

The Cholmondlay Sisters

A late Stuart Hanoverian picture of the British School. This delightful, stylised and detailed painting shows the sisters sitting side by side complete with babies in arms, bows, lace and the whole paraphernalia of the time, depicted in tones of red, pink, yellow, grey and orange.

George Stubbs 1724–1806

The greatest British painter of the horse. His love of nature coupled with intensive anatomical study of his subject led to an unselfconscious artistry in this field of painting. The landscapes behind each animal are filled with surprising groups of plants painted in rich detail. All his best qualities can be seen in ' A Grey Hack with a White Greyhound and Groom '.

William Blake 1757–1827

While working for publishers as an engraver Blake produced poems and watercolour illustrations for books he published himself. His works include *Songs of Innocence, Songs of Experience* and illustrations of the Bible. From an early neo-classical style he turned to an unconventional use of colour, light and form that suited his turbulent visions. *Nebuchadnezzar* is a literal portrayal of the figure described in Daniel 4: 33.

Joseph Turner 1775–1851

One of the most forward-thinking artists of all time, Turner made great use of the brilliancy of coloured light and space, achieving his effects first in watercolour then in oil-paints. His style was a forerunner of a type of impressionism in that he did away with precise form and outline and strict, detailed tonal relationship. The changing moods of nature during sunsets, fogs and storms excited him. This is evident in *Ponte delle Torri, Spoleto*; and the rich qualities of his red, browns and white can be seen in *George IV at a Banquet in Edinburgh*.

Roy Lichtenstein (1923–)

Wham! typifies a style that began with cave paintings and still lives in present day films and comics. The ability of a cartoon to tell a story is the basis of its eternal popularity. *Wham!* is crude, compelling, technically efficient and encapsulates the materialism, commercialism, industrialism and stress of the twentieth century.

Henry Moore (1898–)

Moore is widely accepted as the most eminent semi-abstract sculptor alive today. Early influences were Michelangelo and Mexican sculpture; compare the picture of his 'recumbent figure' with the onyx offering bowl from Mexico (see plate between pages 60–61). Well-known works are drawings of people sleeping in air raid shelters during the last war and the monumental 'Madonna' sculpture in the church at Northampton. His female figures, warriors and recent elephant skull etchings are among the works to be found all over the world.

Ideas for classwork based on visits to the Tate Gallery

1 Study the paintings by Turner and write a short story about a day in the painter's life based on one of these subjects: (a) a morning in the studio, (b) painting by the sea, (c) visiting a prospective buyer.

2 Look at *Poplars on the Epte* or any other paintings by Monet (1840–1926), who was the leading member of the impressionist group in Paris. Find out all you can about impressionism, describe the style and mention any other artists who belonged to the group. Paint a picture using either this technique or the pointillist technique developed by Seurat (1858–91), whose work can also be seen in the gallery.

3 Constable (1776–1837), like Turner, greatly influenced landscape painting in Britain. Look at his pictures, especially *Hampstead Heath with a Rainbow*. What strikes you about the figures and landscapes in his work? In what ways did he depart from previous landscape painting techniques?

4 Look at 'Ophelia' by the pre-Raphaelite Millais (1829–96). What do you think of the artist's rendering of his subject? Who was his model? What is the story connected with her posing for this picture? Read the scene of Ophelia's death in Shakespeare's *Hamlet*. Who were the pre-Raphaelites? Why were they called this?

5 The Russian artist Kandinsky (1866–1944) painted 'improvisations' and 'compositions', moving all the while towards abstraction. He produced an emotional effect from lines, shapes and colours. Look at 'Fragment for Composition IV' and paint your own composition, using the same technique, for one of the following: (a) fear, (b) joy, (c) sorrow, (d) anger.

6 Study the pictures in the gallery by Braque (1882–1963) – one is 'Guitar and Jug'. He and Picasso were the joint inventors of the cubist technique. The jug is divided into two halves to represent form and shapes are reduced to geometrical forms to represent what is seen. Make a painting, a fabric collage or a graphic design on this principle.

7 Study sculpture by Henry Moore, Bernard Meadows and Elizabeth Frink and make a small model of (a) a figure, (b) a bird or (c) an abstract design stimulated by the style and treatment of one of these sculptors.

8 Ceri Richards (1903–71) was greatly influenced by the music of Debussy and made a number of three-dimensional fabric collages in-

spired by *The Cathedral under the Sea*. He also produced lithographs illustrating some of Dylan Thomas's poems and paintings inspired by Trafalgar Square in London, some of which can be seen in the gallery. Which inspires you most when you are making a picture, music, poetry or reality? Make your choice and paint a picture using one of these as a source of inspiration.

9   Study Blake's pictures based on the Bible. Which passages from this book affect you most and fix a picture in your mind? Find the description concerned and make a linocut, an illustration or a painting based on this.

10   In photomontage, photographs are applied to other photographs on an unusual or incongruous background. The technique was often used by 'Cubists' (sticking newspaper cuttings on as well), and used nowadays a great deal by advertising firms. Study as many works, in this style and also in the 'surrealist' style (for fantasy approaches), as possible in the museum (look in books for names you cannot find) designed by Braque (1882–1963), Picasso (1881–1973), Chirico (born 1888), and Salvador Dali (1904–to date).

11   In this gallery, which is your favourite century of painting among these – seventeenth, eighteenth, nineteenth or twentieth? Pick three artists from each one, comment on one work from each, giving the title. Give a brief account of his or her life and find (and name) from books, one musician, one writer, one architect, one craftsman, and one scientist from the same century.

12   Whose sculpture appeals to you the most in the Tate's collection? Give the name, title of work, and a brief account of his or her life.

TOWER OF LONDON   Tower Hill, EC3

Weapons, armour, helmets, medals, uniforms and the Crown Jewels.

Traitor's Gate through which many illustrious prisoners were taken, including Princess Elizabeth when she was imprisoned by Mary I for two months.

Tower Green where several famous people, including queens, were executed. There have always been ravens around the door and legend has it that the Tower will only survive so long as they remain.

White Tower where the oldest church in London, and one of the most beautiful, can be seen: St John's Chapel, a fine piece of Norman architecture. This tower was one of the castles built for William the Conqueror's soldiers.

Bloody Tower where Edward V and Richard of York are believed to have been murdered in 1483. Sir Walter Raleigh was imprisoned here for thirteen years. Sovereigns from William I to James I always stayed at the Tower, which was used as a palace, the night before their coronation.

Beefeaters, or yeoman of the guard, attend the Tower in full costume.

The chief yeoman takes part in the ceremony of the keys each night.

Some exhibits in the Tower of London

Armour

One of the suits of armour on display was worn by Charles II at the age of twelve, when he was Prince of Wales. Another belonged to Henry VIII who, when he was nineteen and slim, wore skirted or tonlet armour but, as he grew older and fatter, needed a very strong horse and equally strong armour. This suit was made at Greenwich, complete with visored helmet, in bright steel. There is also a breastplate worn during the Siege of Malta, with a large hole made by a sword aimed at the stomach. Other exhibitions are helmets from that period, shields and swords.

Medals

Some of Britains most famous awards are among these, including the Victoria Cross (VC), the George Cross (GC), the Distinguished Service Order (DSO), the Distinguished Service Cross (DSC), the Military Cross (MC) and the Distinguished Flying Cross (DFC).

Crowns

After the execution of Charles I many royal ornaments were destroyed by Cromwell, and a new set of Crown Jewels had to be found and made up for Charles II. A crown weighing 2 kg (5 lb), known as St Edward's Crown, was made for him. The frame had escaped the destruction and the jewels may have come from broken crowns. The miniver-trimmed purple velvet cap of estate is inside it. Queen Victoria's diamond crown, little bigger than an apple, is also there; and the crown worn for the Opening of Parliament, which contains the Black Prince's ruby among the 3000 jewels set in its oak-leaf patterned frame. The Koh-i-nor diamond is set in the crown that was made for the present Queen Mother at her coronation in 1937. This gem is supposed to bring good luck to any woman who wears it but bad luck to any man.

Sword of State

The most beautiful and valuable sword in the world, this was made for George IV and is used at all coronations. The hilt and scabbard are of dull gold encrusted with jewels. At the top of the hilt there are four large rubies and a large diamond, below which are many emeralds and diamonds. Lions' heads guard the hand at each end of the crosspiece. In the centre, where the hilt meets the crosspiece, is an immense emerald. There are also sapphires, rubies, smaller emeralds, a large oval turquoise, jewelled laurel sprays, a rose, a thistle, a shamrock and a cross.

State Salt

The decoratively gilded and enamelled State Salt is of Continental manufacture, dating from the sixteenth or seventeenth century, and was used at the coronation given for all monarchs from Charles II to George IV. There are lizards and frogs round the base and gems are set in the silver-gilt.

Ideas for classwork based on visits to the Tower of London

1 Tell the story of the murder of the princes in the Tower in your own words, and illustrate it. Try to describe the characters of the people involved and to convey the fear and guilt felt by the murderers. Ensure that costumes, furniture and interior decorations included in your illustrations are in period.

2 Knights used to keep their all-night vigil before being dubbed in St John's Chapel. Make a sketch of the architecture inside the chapel and the altar and cross, and paint a picture of a Knight of the Bath praying in front of the altar. Try to achieve the correct atmosphere. Would there be candles burning and casting long, perhaps menacing shadows on the columns? Would the knight be cold? tired? frightened? relaxed?

3 Make a fabric collage, a model or a linocut of the Tower of London, with a king in authentic costume, a knight or a yeoman of the guard. Show a part of the Tower where you would expect to find the figure you have chosen.

4 Many armorial banners and flags had heraldic designs showing the family arms or other objects connected with the family. Make a banner or flag as a fabric collage, using four colours and sticking or sewing on a motif you consider appropriate for yourself. Keep the design simple.

5 Make drawings in pen and ink of three decorative sword hilts from (a) a small 'town' sword, (b) a ceremonial or presentation sword and (c) any other sword that interests you.

6 Draw a Viking sword and shield, a Greek sword and shield and an Italian sword and shield. Comment on variations in shape, materials and decoration.

7 Make a large group mural of a medieval tournament, including authentic helmets, armour, arms, horse's armour and trappings, lances, banners, costumes and decorative hangings.

8 Draw a British, French or German knight in full armour. Find out what the different pieces are called and label them all.

9 You can see real ravens on Tower Green and flying round the buildings. Imagine one of them in one of the following periods of history and make a composition with the king, the background, costumes, and, somewhere in the picture, the raven looking on.

(a) In the time of Henry III (who installed three leopards and a polar bear there in the Royal Menagerie), (b) In the time of Henry VIII, (c) In the time of Charles I. All these sovereigns stayed the night there before the coronation, but various other events took place in these reigns as well.

VICTORIA AND ALBERT MUSEUM
Cromwell Road, South Kensington, SW7

Fine and applied arts of all countries, including England, France, Holland, China, Italy, Japan, India, Islam and Spain, periods and styles. Many objects were made to decorate churches, rich merchants' houses or palaces. Arms and armour: swords, helmets, daggers, breastplates. The art of the book. Bronzes, ivory, stone and iron work. Carpets, tapestries and furniture. Development of costume: how clothes were affected by period, transport, furniture and materials. China, pottery and porcelain: Chinese, French, Staffordshire, Wedgwood, majolica, slip-ware, thrown, hand and machine made. Ecclesiastical crafts: stained glass, reredos, wooden carved figures, altar cloths, vestments. Enamels and jewellery: ships made of jewels, rings, necklaces, brooches. Textiles and embroidery: Coptic, French, British, Chinese; development of materials and designs; silk and hair pictures, ' stumpwork ', lace. Oil-paintings, watercolours, drawings (several by Constable), prints and Persian paintings. Old musical instruments, some beautifully shaped and decorated. Glass, pewter, gold and silver work: Italian, Bristol glass, Georgian silver. Theatre art: model theatres and figures, stage design from the eighteenth century to the present day. Rooms with furniture of all periods, (mainly English) including the newly designed galleries displaying the Jones collection of eighteenth-century furniture, ceramics, glass, silver, tapestries and other exhibits.

* *Apply to Assistant Keeper, Education Department.* Art and crafts demonstration room. Drama lectures and activities. Saturday morning club. Courses. Holiday programmes.

Some exhibits in the Victoria and Albert Museum
Three leather panels (Jones collection)
Panels like these were made in England and Holland in the eighteenth century by covering the surface with silver or tinfoil and then coating it with golden-yellow varnish. Here, painted Chinese figures and houses, in various colours, practically cover the background. Chinoiserie of this type was very popular at the time.

Chamber of mirrors (Jones collection)
A delightful little Italian room (1780), with the walls and ceiling made of glass and decorated in gold relief and white paint. When candles were alight on the tables their flames were reflected in the mirrors.

Weathercock
This French eighteenth-century ' cockerill ' made from wrought iron and

copper has some very interesting patterning which is worth studying for adaptation for linocuts, embroidery, tile design and fabric or paper collage. Small, similar-patterned, various-sized shapes are repeated to form the stylised body feathers; longer, somewhat similar shapes are repeated in various sizes for the magnificent swirling tail. The simplified beak, comb and eye are also interesting, as is the pose – one leg raised, the other planted firmly on the ground. The amazing length of the talons helps to support the large body.

The Good Shepherd

A seventeenth- or eighteenth-century Indo-Chinese carving, wonderfully detailed and skilfully made from an elephant's tusk. The Tree of Life spreads its branches at the top, with God, the Christ child and a dove sitting in the centre. Beneath is a rectangular shape containing three circles: in the first are Mary, Joseph and a fountain; in the second, rabbits, tigers, monkeys and dogs; and in the third, sheep with their lambs, their fleece indicated by a criss-cross pattern.

Chessmen

These are nineteenth-century Chinese red-stained and natural white ivory. Members of Chinese royalty represent our kings, queens, knights and bishops, some on horseback, others on elephants or standing regally with swords and fans. The other chessmen are on horses. All the pieces are mounted on richly decorated supports.

Cream jugs

In the silver gallery there are two pairs of these jugs, one made from silver, the other from silver gilt, in the shape of cows. Cream is poured from the mouth, the handle is the tail, and a fly on the back can be lifted to reveal a hole through which the jug is filled. Shapes and designs were made by heating, moulding, cutting, engraving and sometimes beating the silver and silver gilt. The cows carry the hallmark of John Schuppe and were made soon after 1760.

Beds

The very popular wooden ' Bed of Ware ' was made in England around 1580. It was related that four couples could sleep in it. In the nineteenth century the bed travelled from one inn to another as an object of curiosity. Those who slept in it carved their initials or impressed their seals on the frame. Sir Toby Belch, in Shakespeare's *Twelfth Night*, mentions the bed, and Byron refers to it in *Don Juan*. In contrast to this massive piece of furniture there is a beautiful, tiny, carved and gilded beechwood bed made by George Jacob (Jones collection). The original silk damask curtains, which match the cover, are draped over it. The room where it is displayed is furnished with a French commode and secretaire; mirrors and Chinese candlesticks hang on the deep blue velvet walls.

Glass gallery
This contains a varied collection of blown, cut and moulded glass in colours that include red, blue, pink, green and yellow. Some items are engraved and gilded. Many are moulded with variations of coloured and opaque glass. There are goblets with enamelled twists in the stem, plates, bowls, jugs, glasses of all shapes and sizes and even a tiny mouse made in clear glass. One of the most interesting exhibits is an eighteenth-century beaker and cover made in Bohemia. The clear glass has swirled ruby and *aventurine* enclosures cut on the wheel.

Oil-paintings, watercolours, drawings and prints
There are some very fine oil-paintings and watercolours by Constable and other famous artists. Temporary exhibitions of prints are often held. A particularly interesting one was *Homage to Senefelder*, the German engraver who invented the art of lithography, or surface printing, in 1798. This included: Graham Sutherland's *The Bird* (three colours on white) and *Two Standing Figures* (suggesting part landscape, part plant shapes making up the figures); *Ram's Head* by Picasso, one of his finest prints drawn in 1945; Rouault's *Clowns* and *Crucifixion*, both vivid reflections of sorrow; and Henry Moore's *Seated Figures in Stone*, a bold, sculptural drawing.

Ideas for classwork based on visits to the Victoria and Albert Museum
1 Find the following exhibits: (a) a large wooden sculpture of Christ riding on a donkey, (b) a T'ang horse, (c) a pottery owl, (d) a bird in a piece of seventh to tenth-century Christian Near East weaving. Draw your favourite and write a short history about it, describing its medium and saying why you particularly like it.
2 Illustrate: (a) a Victorian outdoor dress, (b) a Victorian evening dress. Describe the materials from which each is made.
3 Find one of the following: (a) a face from the Syon embroidered cope, (b) a face from Chinese embroidery, (c) a face from seventeenth-century stumpwork. Use it, adding the rest of the figure if you like, as the basis for a two- or three-dimensional (ie padded) fabric collage.
4 Find and draw three different types of each of the following: (a) collars, (b) cuffs, (c) shoes. These can be copied from costume models, embroidery or pictures. State which periods they date from.
5 Find four different patterns, one from each of the following: (a) stonework, (b) woodwork, (c) ceramics, (d) ironwork. Draw a section of each one and make an abstract painting based on one of them.
6 Look at the jewellery section and design a ring or brooch using

a ruby, two emeralds and four turquoises set in gold or silver.

7 Find and draw a picture of the Virgin and Child in each of the following media: (a) ivory, (b) wood, (c) stone, (d) silver. Make a figure in clay based on one of them. Look for simplification of the faces, folds in the dress, expressions of tenderness and positioning of the arms.

8 Look for pictures or small sculptured figures of kings. Make a model of a king from cardboard cylinders, egg boxes, tinsel, silver, gold and coloured papers or fabrics, sequins and coloured beads.

9 Make a papier mâché plate and decorate it with one of the following: (a) a bird in a circle of flowers, (b) a tiger surrounded by jungle leaves, (c) a fish in a circle of waterweeds. Study the plates in the museum to help you. Plates are treated in much the same way as posters which have to present a simple motif and a clearly defined pattern.

10 Make a padded fabric collage based on the seventeenth-century stumpwork pictures. Use cotton wool, sponge or pieces of felt for the padding.

11 Make sketches of: (a) a statue of Buddha, (b) a bronze figure of Shiva, (c) a red sandstone figure of Sri (goddess of wealth). Using one of these, paint a figure placing the figure in an appropriate landscape or interior, surrounded by people in Indian costume, praying.

12 Study some ecclesiastical designs and make a stained glass window with coloured cellophane for glass, sequins or beads for the jewel-like glitter of sun-rays, haloes and costumes and black paper for the leading. Choose either an abstract motif that conveys the feelings and colours of the Resurrection, or a representational design of the figure of Christ in heaven or the Devil in hell.

13 Make an embroidered hanging, using fabric collage, wool or silk, after the fashion of the Stuart examples; but instead of Charles I and Henrietta Maria, choose another king and queen and place them in a garden with lions, trees, fruit, flowers and butterflies. Study pictures of the king and queen to give guidance over costume and appearance.

14 Look for (a) a linocut, (b) a lithograph, (c) an etching. Explain how one of them has been made. Give the title, the date and the artist's name.

15 There is great variety in the stems of the glasses on display. Find out what the following terms mean: (a) four spiral gauzes, (b) lace twist outlined, (c) multi-ply corkscrew, (d) two-ply spiral band. Draw a part of the pattern used in each and write the name under each one.

16 Write a description of one of the following:
(a) a winged goblet, Hawley Bishopp, seventeenth century, (b) a jug in soda metal, heavily crizzled, Ravenscroft, seventeenth century, (c) a panel-moulded bowl on a seventeenth-century wine glass, (d) a goblet with cypher, Baluster glass, (e) a satin glass spill vase in shaded blue

and silver, English, seventeenth century, (f) a figure in coloured pâté de verre, Nevers, seventeenth century.

17 Study the theatre section and if possible visit the Pollock Toy Theatre and Museum (1 Scala Street, London W1) with a friend to compare the different methods of treatment. ' Penny plain and tuppence coloured ' were designed by Pollock in the nineteenth century. Suggest ideas for your own play, the characters, and types of costume they should wear. Make your own toy theatre, scenery and figures.

18 Divide the class into study groups; from the following ideas make a book about the history of tapestry using sketches and paintings of interesting designs.

(a) Babylon examples taken from temples and palaces.

(b) Egyptian tapestries removed from ancient tombs.

(c) Red Indian tapestry in America.

(d) Tapestries from the Middle Ages which covered walls and entrances and commemorated battles.

(e) Belgian and Flemish tapestries – used for kings' palaces – and the Vatican in Rome.

(f) Modern Asian tapestries.

(g) Present day Gobelin tapestries from France – used in churches. (The factory here made the tapestry for Coventy Cathedral from the design by Graham Sutherland.)

19 Imagine the listed people have been asked to choose a favourite object from the museum in one of the following media. Choose an appropriate object made from each medium, describe it, say when it was designed, and if known for what purpose it was used. Why did you pick the object for the particular person named?

(a) Napoleon, (b) Madame Curie, (c) Inigo Jones, (d) Elizabeth Fry, (e) Michelangelo, (f) Henrietta Maria, (g) Charles Dickens

Media: marble, silver, wood, precious stones, pottery, glass, tapestry.

WALLACE COLLECTION Hertford House, Manchester Square, W1

Eighteenth-century furnished rooms, carpets, miniatures, Renaissance (classical revival) and medieval paintings of British, Dutch and French schools. European arms and armour. Sixteenth-century porcelain and majolica. Bronze and gold work. Eighty-nine small boxes, among them two from Paris made in gold and enamel, one in the form of a coach seat, the other shell-shaped with white peacock feather decorations.

Some exhibitions in the Wallace Collection

Watteau 1684–1721

The painting *Les Charmes de la Vie* epitomises the delight and frivolity of the eighteenth century in France. Watteau captured the dainty poses of the women's elegant heads, particularly the shapely back views. He worked in Paris for a year with Gillot, a theatrical scenery painter, and then moved on to work with the Keeper of the Luxembourg Palace. The formation of his style began with hundreds of drawings of figures, heads, hands and draperies that he made as a consequence of his stay there and used over and over again in his paintings. He achieved fame as a painter of *fêtes galantes*, and, because of the constant use of his original drawings, all his paintings have a strong family likeness.

Swords and rapiers

Three of these are particularly fine and ornamental.

1 Prince Henry's sword

Prince Henry's type of sword, of medieval design and cross-hilted, was revived during the seventeenth century when James I reintroduced the ancient ceremony of creating Knights of the Bath. The knight-to-be knelt before the monarch who tapped him gently on each shoulder with the sword.

2 Presentation sword

Very intricate and fine craftsmanship: the hilt is made of solid gold with designs picked out in red, blues and white. It was presented by the East India Company to Lieutenant James Hartley, for gallantry during the Mahratta War in 1779.

3 Seventeenth-century rapier

This elaborately designed rapier has a hilt to protect the swordsman's hand. Minutely chiselled relief gives it the appearance of a detailed piece of sculpture.

Silver mounted gun

Made in 1735 and said to have belonged to George II, this airgun displays very intricate decoration and wonderful craftsmanship. The steel stock shows the figure of Jupiter brandishing a thunderbolt with foliage in chiselled relief. The carved walnut stock is inlaid with silver.

Jean Henry Riesener

An eighteenth-century craftsman who made all types of furniture under the patronage of the French Crown for ten years. Marie Antoinette continued to order designs by him right up to the Revolution. He specialised in highly elaborate marquetry (veneers of various coloured woods) in geometrical designs. The Dutch introduced this form of decoration in the late seventeenth century and bird, flower and foliage designs were used, often with the addition of bone and ivory.

Eighty-nine boxes

These beautiful little eighteenth-century boxes, in various shapes and sizes, typify some of the French approaches to design and colour and include some items of great rarity. With the boxes are some rich examples of Renaissance jewellery.

Sèvres porcelain
In 1756 the factory that first made 'soft paste' porcelain at Vincennes was transferred to Sèvres; it is still there today. Later a new 'hard paste' porcelain was introduced. The most characteristic pieces of Sèvres ware are decorated with paintings enclosed in panels. Some of the coloured grounds are particularly famous: 1752 turquoise; 1753 yellow; 1756 pea-green; 1757 rose pompadour; and finally bleu de roi. Design consisted of landscapes, figures and festoons of flowers. Later, translucent or tinted reliefs were invented, but these were not of the same quality as the earlier decorations. Two of the eighty-nine boxes mentioned above are from Sèvres.

Gothic horse armour
A very fine late fifteenth-century armoured rider and horse, imaginatively displayed.

Ideas for classwork based on visits to the Wallace Collection
1   Decide which is your favourite among the eighty-nine small boxes. Describe its shape, the materials used to make it, its colour and its decoration. State when and where it was made.
2   Compare a French marble or bronze bust from the Wallace Collection with one from another country that you have seen in another museum or in a book. Say which you prefer and why.
3   Study women's hair and costumes in pictures around the museum. Describe the hair, clothes, shoes and hats belonging to your two favourite styles.
4   Compare a piece of Sèvres porcelain with any piece of English porcelain you have seen in a museum or a book.
5   What is majolica? Find an exhibit made in this medium, describe at and paint part of a design from it.
6   There are many examples of goldsmiths' work here. Choose three, compare the pieces, and say which one you think is the best in terms of truth to the medium, design and workmanship.
7   Set up and paint a still-life group based on things you have learnt from the pictures in the museum.

WHITWORTH ART GALLERY Whitworth Park, Manchester

Department of paintings, sculpture and drawings: modern continental artists – Gauguin, Van Gogh, Cézanne, Picasso, Klee; English artists – Gainsborough, Turner, Sutherland; sculptors – Moore, Frink, Hepworth.

Department of prints: British, Japanese, Italian and German Renaissance. Depart of textiles: British, Egyptian, Greek and German.

Some exhibits from the Whitworth Art Gallery
The Twin Towers of the Sfinx-State
Patterned piston-shaped towers, rectangles and a circle made in bronze: sculpture by Eduardo Paolozzi (1924–). It is interesting to compare this medium and patterning with the 'Whitworth Tapestry' (wool and Terylene) designed by him and woven by the Edinburgh Tapestry Co. He also works in concrete, water colour, collage and ceramics.

Mount Fuji
Coloured woodprint by the famous Japanese artist Katsushika Hokusi (1760–1849). A beautifully composed picture with the boat shape designed so that it crosses the print from the top left-hand corner to the bottom right-hand corner, birds and grass filling in the left-hand space and a mountain in the right-hand space. Lovely textures and patterns and a figure pouring water over the side of the boat.

Greek Island (Parga) pillow cover
A seventeenth-century silk embroidery on linen. Decorative and exciting in design. Two lively figures, flowers and trees, with an attractive border.

Egyptian cover fragment
Tapestry of woven wool and linen dating from the fourth or fifth century AD. Mounted horseman and four kneeling figures, each inside a circle.

Hannah Smith's embroidered casket
Seventeenth-century silk, gilt and silver embroidery on satin, with figures, animals, buildings, flowers and trees. Well-bred young ladies living in this century frequently embroidered the strips themselves (graduating from samplers and pictures), and cabinet makers assembled them, adding handles, drawers, and mirrors, to make caskets for personal belongings and jewellery.

Ideas for classwork based on visits to the Whitworth Art Gallery
1 Look at the embroidered boxes. Cover a cardboard box for yourself with figures, animals, flowers and trees cut out from magazines, varnish it and add sequins, beads or shells if you have any. This will make an attractive container for necklaces, bracelets and brooches.

2 Study the Greek Island pillow cover. This could give you ideas for an appliquèd bed cover, using figures (perhaps in modern dress) with stylised flowers and trees, or flowers and trees treated in a more abstract fashion. Materials used should be washable, with dyes well fixed.

3 Find: (a) the bronze sculpture *Beast* by Lynn Chadwick (1914–), (b) the sculpture in wood *torso* by Barbara Hepworth (1903–), (c) the Flemish fifteenth-century oak carving *Deposition*. Which do you prefer? Why? Describe your choice.

4 Compare the painting *Search* (emulsion on board) by Bridget Riley (1931–) with the woodcut *Dazzle Camouflage, Ship in Dry Dock 1918* by William Wadsworth (1889–1949).

5 Look for these wood-engravings: (a) *The Hansom Cab and the Pigeons* by Eric Ravilious, (b) *Gossip* by Iain Macnab, (c) *Jonah Cast to the Waves* by David Jones.
Compare them and say which is your favourite and why? Which do you consider the most modern in design?

6 Look at the paintings, prints, textiles and embroideries in the museum and use ideas derived from them to design the following: (a) outdoor wear, (b) indoor day-wear, (c) party wear. Make sketches, stating colours and materials to be used.

7 Choose one of the following sections: (a) embroidery, (b) prints, (c) painting, (d) sculpture, (e) dress, textile or wallpaper design, (f) sculpture. Study the exhibits. Imagine that you are about to leave school and you want to study art or craft at college. Write a letter to the Principal, inventing or adding to your qualifications and describing your knowledge of the subject and your ideas about it. The Principal (ie form teacher) is given the letters and they are read to and discussed with a panel of staff from the art school (chosen from the class): a sculptor, a painter, a designer, an illustrator and an embroiderer. The best letters secure an interview. One student can be accepted from each section.

8 Select any three objects and use them in a design for a Christmas card for the museum.

9 Choose an exhibit (dramatic, amusing or decorative) which you would like to see on a poster for the museum. How would you use it in a design, what lettering would you choose, and what background colour?

10 The Whitworth Art Gallery has had many splendid loan exhibitions. Describe one you have seen and liked and suggest something you would like in the future. These ideas might help – the past, contemporary, fine art, craft, British, foreign, older generation, younger generation, mixed or one man exhibitions from the past or the present.

SCOTLAND

CITY ART GALLERY AND MUSEUM Kelvingrove, Glasgow

Art gallery: British, French, Dutch and Italian paintings. Archaeology and history: ethnography. Costume. Glass and stained glass. Armour. Furniture. Ship models. Natural history.

*   *Apply to Museums Education Officer.* Annual art competition. Saturday art club. Evening classes.

Some exhibits from the City Art Gallery and Museum, Glasgow

Fifteenth-century French tapestry
Sumptuous millefleurs motif: a field of flowers with Charity on an elephant brandishing a sword and about to strike Envy.

Court ladies of the Chinese T'ang period
Court ladies with head-dresses and ornate costume. Tomb figures of people, birds and animals, made from terracotta, bronze and glazed earthenware.

Enamel spur
Enamelled brass was the fashion at the beginning of the Restoration. The popular blue and white opaque enamels were applied in the recessed sections of low-relief designs. This crane-neck spur includes a sculptural flower design.

Flintlock pistols
Used for self-defence or hunting, these decorative seventeenth-century German pistols were carried in holsters slung on either side of a horse's saddle.

The Rehearsal by Edgar Degas
French painter, sculptor and print maker (1834–1917). His principal subjects were ballet girls, models (bathing, dressing, ironing) and carabet artists. He was interested in the portrayal of light, colour, form and movement. In later years, when his eyesight weakened, he made greater use of pastels and these gave broader, freer effects.

Ideas for classwork based on visits to the City Art Gallery and Museum, Glasgow

1   Which is your favourite piece of Gothic art? Describe it.
2   What is the story of HMS *Hood*? Write your own version and illustrate it.
3   Choose one artist from each of the following centuries, name and describe a picture he painted, and then say which one is your favourite out of the five: (a) sixteenth, (b) seventeenth, (c) eighteenth, (d) nineteenth, (e) twentieth.
4   Pick one object made from each of the following:
(a) bronze, (b) glass, (c) porcelain, (d) silver, (e) cotton.
Make up a story in which all these things play a part and illustrate it with a picture of one of them in use.

Holiday competition *Watch The Birdie*
Child taking a portrait photograph with a polaroid instamatic camera in a studio specially set up at the National Portrait Gallery

Practical work in the Children's Gallery to learn about weights
Crown copyright   Science Museum, London

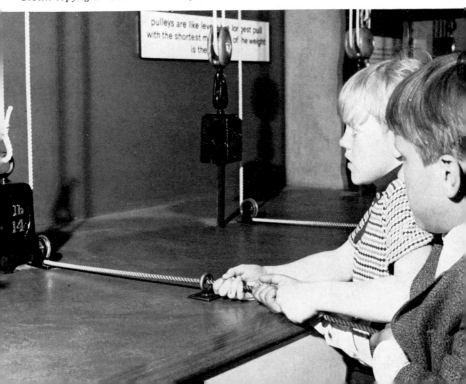

Bronze-gilt statue of Vajrapani from Tibet
E. M. Scratton Collection on loan to Ashmolean Museum, Oxford

5   Imagine you have travelled in the *Queen Mary* and that you are one of the following: (a) a film star, (b) successful businessman, (c) ship's officer, (d) ship's hairdresser, (e) ship's photographer. Make up a story about one day on board, describing: (a) your cabin, (b) food, (c) entertainment, (d) people you met, (e) shops on board, (f) scenery.

6   Look at an example of stained glass from the Burrell collection. How many colours have been used? What holds the pieces of glass in place? Make an abstract or figurative fabric collage with a stained-glass effect using black felt, string, wool or braid with coloured, textured materials.

7   Choose one exhibit from each of the following categories, study them and take notes: (1) pottery, (2) prints, (3) textiles or rugs, (4) costumes, (5) sculpture, (6) painting, (7) silverware, (8) jewellery. Pick two panels, each with four members. Elect a questioner who puts a question to each panel in turn, dealing with the following aspects of each item: (a) shape, (b) texture, (c) colour, (d) pattern, (e) composition, (f) medium, (g) history, (h) the artist or craftsman if known, (i) date. Award points for each correct answer and declare the panel with the highest collective score the winner.

8   Look at abstract pattern work on textiles, vases or anything else in the museum and make sketches of the patterns you consider most attractive. Use these to make a design on canvas, experimenting with different textures such as silks, wools, rafia, leather and string, and making sure the stitching is securely fastened off on the back.

9   You are arranging an exhibition at the museum entitled ' The spirit of Glasgow and her surroundings '. This can be set long ago or in the present day. Describe one exhibit, which can be either something you have seen in the Museum or something imaginary which you would like to include in each of the following sections:
(a) pleasure steamers, (b) fishing, (c) botany, (d) natural history, (e) art, (f) craft, (g) geology, (h) entertainment, (i) shops.

10   Choose and describe one of the following objects, and make up a story pretending you were the person who found it and presented it to the museum.
(a) a goblet, (b) a plate, (c) jewellery, (d) a statue, (e) a tapestry, (f) a costume.

NATIONAL MUSEUM OF ANTIQUITIES OF SCOTLAND
Queen Street, Edinburgh

Stone, Bronze and Iron Ages. Treasures from graves of the Vikings. Coins and medals. Weapons and working implements. Costumes and photographs.
Relics: Sir Walter Scott, Robert Burns and others.

F

△ *Apply to Schools Museum Officer, South Bridge School, Infirmary Street, Edinburgh.*

Some exhibits in the National Museum of Antiquities of Scotland

Medieval oak panel

Decorative panel (early sixteenth century) from the Abbott Panter's hospital in Montrose, made by craftsmen in eastern Scotland. Carved stylised thistles, leaves and birds with standing friars satirically represented with the heads, legs and tails of foxes but wearing traditional religious clothing.

Roman helmet

Parade helmet with visor-mask showing realistic features (nose, mouth and chin) with slits for the eyes. The headpiece shows curls and side-pieces. Dates from the Flavian period, AD 80–100.

Biblical flask

One of more than a hundred objects brought back to Britain by northern pirates and buried at Traprain Law. Scenes depicting Adam and Eve and the Adoration of the Virgin and Child can be seen round the base of this fourth-century flask.

Single-stilted wooden plough

Nineteenth-century farming implement from Shetland. This has a sculptural appearance and might give ideas for abstract work based on *objets trouvés*.

Tartan collection

This includes letters and patterns of Wilson of Bannockburn, tartan weavers in the late eighteenth century.

Dress collection

This ranges from the eighteenth century to the twentieth and includes dresses, hats, underwear, shoes, stockings and gloves. There is even information about some of the wearers. Photographs give some idea of the social setting in which the clothes were worn.

Ideas for classwork based on visits to the National Museum of Antiquities of Scotland

1   Look at the ' Penicuik jewels ' belonging to Mary, Queen of Scots and compare her necklace with a necklace from the Bronze Age in terms of texture, design and colour.

2   Describe your favourite examples from each of the following types of ornament: (a) brooches, (b) hair fillets, (c) rings.

3   Make your own fashion pages for an imaginary magazine, comparing

articles of clothing from two different centuries, amusing, entertaining or instructive comments may be added. Choose three items from among the following: (a) gloves or gauntlets, (b) hats, (c) shoes, (d) dresses, (e) underwear.

4 Sketch objects made from three of the following materials: (a) enamel, (b) silver, (c) bronze, (d) stone, (e) wood, (f) wool. Make up a thriller story about one of these objects, set in the appropriate century. Describe costumes, buildings and food to give added authenticity.

5 Study the coins and pick out your favourite famous person from among those they portray. Describe the way he or she has been depicted by the artist, and give a summary of his or her life.

6 Look at the domestic ware in the museum. Find as many examples as possible of any *one* item, for instance plates, bowls, drinking cups or jugs. Draw them, say what material was used for them, date them and give their place of origin. If you have less than four examples, go to your school or local library and find two more.

7 Look at the medals and coins and see if you can find horses, lions, unicorns or any other animals on them. Use an idea from one of them to make a fabric collage or machine-embroidered picture in three colours.

8 There are several 'personal relics' in the museum. Find the relic belonging to each of the following: (a) Prince Charles Edward Stuart, (b) Sir Walter Scott, (c) Lady Grizell, (d) Alexander Selkirk, (e) Robert Burns. Choose items from two of the following categories which might be considered suitable 'personal relics' of yourself and describe them both: (a) furniture, (b) clothing, (c) ornament.

9 Look for lockets in the museum. Find an old photograph or portrait from a magazine, some pictures of jewels or beads and some silver or gold paper; with these design a locket mounted on a contrasting background (black, red or green paper). You can add sequins or real beads as well.

10 Find out all you can about the lighting appliances on display in the museum, and make a cartoon illustrating the different methods of lighting you have seen, giving their dates.

11 Study the photographs in the dress collection. How has the art of photography changed over the years with regard to (a) composition, (b) invention of different cameras and (c) tone and colour? Which is your favourite picture in the collection and why?

WALES

NATIONAL MUSEUM OF WALES Cathays Park, Cardiff

Archaeology: prehistory of Wales's excavations, Iron Age. Botany: fungi, seaweeds, plants, flowers. Geology: rocks, minerals, fossils. Zoology:

invertebrates, fishes, reptiles, mammals, birds. Industry: ships, mining, iron, steel, glass, gas.
* *Apply to Schools Service Officer.*

Some exhibits in the National Museum of Wales
Bronze triton
A sea-god, man's head and torso, with fish's tail, by Severo da Ravenna (Padua, fifteenth century).

Dolgellau chalice
Dating from the thirteenth century, this chalice is one of the earliest examples of church plate in Britain. It has a shallow bowl, a lobed knot halfway up the stem, and leaf-shaped designs on the foot.

Nantgarw porcelain ice-pail
Milky-white porcelain decorated with birds, flowers and trees, and forming part of a large dessert service made c 1817–20.

Bronze plaque
This plaque 150–50 BC was found at Lyn Cerrig Bach, Anglesey, and illustrates the skill of the early Celts in metal work. The embossed 'triskele' pattern is designed in the middle part of the plaque. This type of bold primitive shape and decoration inspires many of today's young jewellery craftsmen.

Sea mats
The Bugula are fan-shaped compartments resembling sea-weeds, each containing an individual animal, and are a common sight around the Welsh coast.

Comma Butterfly
One of the many beautifully coloured creatures which can be seen in the Welsh countryside. It was originally to be found mainly in Monmouthshire.

Ideas for classwork based on visits to the National Museum of Wales
1 Make a booklet about Wales using information you have found in the National Museum. Divide it into the following sections: (a) art, (b) archaeology, (c) botany, (d) geology, (e) industry, (f) zoology. Draw a picture of one object mentioned in each section, using felt tips, wax crayons or whatever you think will give the best results.
2 Divide the class into four groups and make a wall chart of flowers and plants which bloom in the spring, summer, autumn and winter, based on exhibits in the museum's botany section.

3   Look at the various Celtic crosses and adapt one to make a modern brooch. Say how you would make it up (using gold, silver, enamel, jewels, and so on) and do a rough sketch of it with notes.

4   Study the models of the Roman fort and villa. Choose one or the other and describe the people you would have seen there when it was first built and the clothes they would have worn. Find out about and sketch their cooking utensils, weapons and toys.

5   Use your favourite fossil plant or section to make a scarf from a sketched design, using the batik method.

6   Go and look at the current special exhibition. Imagine you are an art critic on a newspaper and write a review mentioning:

(a) the title of the exhibition, (b) three favourite exhibits, with full descriptions, names of designers and dates if known, (c) Your opinion of the display, (d) anything else which would make readers want to go and look round.

7   Look at the sculptured or painted portraits of eminent Welsh men and women. Select your favourite, and describe:

(a) the person, mentioning the name and a few details about his or her life and achievements; (b) the medium used for the portrait, stating which features have been emphasised, whether the finished sculpture or painting gives an idea of strength, integrity, wisdom or other qualities; give the name of the sculptor or painter and dates.

8   Build up a collage, using old matches, ice cream sticks, spoons, dried peas, and other suitable materials, based on patterns found in rock, mine and quarry structures.

9   Sketch your favourite mammal from the Welsh countryside, and make a fabric collage, embroidered picture, painting, linocut, or pottery tile from the idea. Make up a very short poem (which need not rhyme) about it, describing its colour, movements, habits, and so on.

10   Who is your favourite among the Welsh artists whose work is shown in this museum? Write a short biography and say why you like the pictures.

4 Ideas for class work based on visits to local museums

1   Make a form scrapbook with each pupil contributing a favourite black-and-white or colour postcard or a photograph from a guide book. Ask each child to write a short essay on the object he or she has chosen and select someone to write an introduction about the museum building.
2   Look for sculptures in your local museum depicting people who have made local or national history. Choose the one you like best and write an essay on the sculpture, the medium and the skill of the sculptor; include a short description of the man or woman in question.
3   Make a sketch of one of the following: (a) an eighteenth-century steam carriage, (b) a nineteenth-century motor coach, (c) a nineteenth-century locomotive. Fill the vehicle with people in the costume of the period carrying, holly, Christmas trees and presents, and use this in a simplified form as a linocut design for a Christmas card.
4   Study decorative architectural features in your local museum. Make a list of the animals and figures portrayed there and then try to find similar figures on or inside churches or other old buildings in the district.
5   You are on a desert island and want to paint a picture of the landscape or make a sculpture of one of the birds or animals. What materials would you find on the island from which you could make paints and brushes, or which you could use for carving or modelling?
6   Look for museum postcards showing jugs, plates, brooches and other objects with decorative patterning. Cut them up and use them after the style of the Milanese surrealist artist Guiseppe Arcimboldi, who created fantastic faces out of fruit, flowers, vegetables and pieces of landscape, to make eyes, noses, mouths, hair, hats, ears and faces for side or frontal portraits. Black-and-white cards can be just as decorative as coloured ones and can be used effectively on coloured paper. It helps to draw the outline of face and features first as a rough guide.
7   Find and sketch one of the following devices used on flags and coats-of-arms: (a) a griffin, (b) a tiger, (c) a sea-dog, (d) an antelope. Use either the head or the whole body as the theme for a linocut picture on paper or fabric. Leave space for a border and base the design for this on one of the leaf patterns in the plant section, which include *sagittate*

(arrow-like), *hastate* (spear-like), *palmatifid* (palm-like), *pedatisect* (divided like feet), *digitate* (finger-like) and *ternate* (in threes).

8   Look at abstract patterns on plates and designs on architectural fragments, carpets and wood carvings. Choose your favourite and adapt it as a linocut for a greetings card. Use two or three colours, or one colour on coloured paper.

9   Study mosaics in your local museum and make a mosaic design with cut up or torn and painted strips of paper. Do a portrait of a famous king, writer or artist in this medium. Add gold and silver for extra richness and emphasis.

10   Make an abstract collage using spaghetti, dried peas, dried beans, sago and other suitable kitchen products. Use a magnified diatom (a tiny speck of life in the sea), a magnified section of a fruit or a magnified head of an insect as a basis for the design. Drawings and photographs of these can be found in most marine biology, science or natural history sections.

11   Compare Chinese and Persian paintings. Illustrate the differences with reproductions, photographs, drawings and paintings which can show, for example, a detail like variations in the presentation of hands.

12   Find a ' personal relic ' in your local museum and write a short story about it in keeping with its period. Say when it was originally used, where it came from and what you know of the man or woman it belonged to.

13   Artists' freely drawn sketches often appeal to people more than their finished paintings. Why do you think this is? Give examples.

14   The South Sea Islanders carved strange figures which were placed on the prows of their fishing canoes to please the fish so that they would let themselves be caught and cooked. They also made figures from coloured feathers stitched on to wickerwork frames, with pieces of mother-of-pearl for eyes. Make your own unusual figure using some of the materials mentioned and any others you require.

15   Try to find some seventeenth-century hair pictures in a museum. These were made with coloured human hair instead of thread and depicted cottages, people and cows in fields and similar subjects. Try to make a very small picture in the same way. If you do not like using real hair, use nylon, silk or coloured threads.

16   There may be some nineteenth-century tinsel pictures in your local museum: study them. One of the best examples is called *St George and the Dragon*. Sometimes prints were decorated with tinsel. Make a picture with a linoprint and colour some parts with watercolours and others with metallic sweet papers, sequins and feathers.

16   The most interesting English lace bobbins were made during the sixteenth to the nineteenth centuries, most of them from bone and wood but some from silver, pewter, brass, glass and ivory. Plain, slim, straight bobbins were known as ' old maids '. Those with bands and dots of pewter were called respectively Bedfordshire tigers and leopards. Wooden

bobbin shafts were incised and coloured with wording on them such as 'I love you', 'I want a husband' and 'God bless you'. Births, deaths and weddings were recorded and bobbins were sold at public hangings as late as 1861. Coloured beads, buttons and tiny medals were wired on in a loop at the bottom to weight the bobbin and prevent it rolling over on the lace pillows that were made. Make one of your own, using a plastic or bone crochet hook, for St Valentine's Day, Christmas, Easter or a birthday.

17   Divide the class into six sections and make some group murals, in paint, paper or fabric collage, assign to each group a subject connected with one of the following ancient civilisations: (a) Greece, (b) Egypt, (c) Persia, (d) China, (e) Africa, (f) New Zealand.

18   In embroidery the much-criticised fashion for using hollyhocks, crinoline ladies and cottages in popular designs seems to have been replaced by a liking for designs based on organic forms and sections. These are equally open to criticism when taken to excess. Comment on the thought 'the artist who jumps on the bandwagon of fashion puts at risk the production of work of real integrity'. How do you account for the popularity of the old and the new fashions?

19   Embroidery designers, like other artists, either: (a) reflect the inventions, social history, sorrows and joys of the times they live in; (b) present their idea of the future; (c) use old themes in a contemporary way, in terms of design or in the use of new materials and techniques; (d) join the current vogue. Which seems to you to be the most interesting way of visualising and working, and why?

20   Look round your museum for an exceptionally good, interesting and unusual display. Describe it and the effects it has on the object or objects it is setting off.

21   Find out all you can about your local museum: who was responsible for it in the first place? when was it started? what kind of exhibits does it house? Make sketches of any three interesting architectural features it possesses, and of three of your favourite exhibits.

22   If you were starting a museum what objects would you specialise in? (These can be unusual and the museum can be the only one of its kind.) What kind of building would you choose? What kind of interior decoration would you have and how would you arrange some of the displays? Make sketches to illustrate your ideas.

23   Pick out from objects or pictures six hats or head-dresses that catch your eye, each fulfilling one of the following descriptions: (a) regal, (b) smart, (c) amusing, (d) primitive, (e) beautiful, (f) decorative. Make a sketch of each one.

24   Select four hairstyles which appeal to you. How would you adapt one of these for your idea for a fashion trend next year? Which clothes would you adapt or design to go with it? What kind of make-up, jewel-

lery and shoes? Make colour sketches remembering that colours are also subject to fashion. Choose the fabrics from which the clothes would be made.

25 Look for the following items in museums which have collections of costumes, shoes and jewellery: (a) a French hood, (b) a carcanet, (c) a capuchon, (d) a fibula, (e) bekes, (f) a buff coat, (g) falling bands, (h) a bourrelet, (i) a ruff, (j) a stomacher, (k) a cracowe, (l) a crespine. Sketch four of these.

26 You are going to advertise your local museum on television, the time factor to be decided by the teacher or director. Divide the class into groups of three; one in each group is the artist, one the actor and one the producer. Make a large frame out of paper or cardboard, big enough to show the live figure behind it and any visual aids that will be used, to represent the television screen. There are many different ways of advertising; here are some to start you off:

(1) The actor gives a commentary while holding up a large reproduction of an exhibit which is typical of the Museum.

(2) Several ideas can be presented in quick succession by using postcards from the Museum.

(3) Display a painting of the front of the museum, with children going into it looking pleased and interested and the actor reporting what they are saying, or the children can be coming out of it and the actor can quote their comments.

(4) Make use of large lettering, a heading ' Museum ' and a cartoon.

(5) Photographs taken by the group can be used or, in schools where cine cameras are available, a short film can be made.

Each group shows its advertisement to the class who award marks (up to 3: good, medium, poor) for each of these points: (a) presentation (pleasing design), (b) originality, (c) final effect (whether the advertisement makes the audience feel that their museum is an exciting, interesting and worthwhile place to visit, where they will learn something new about life and where they will want to go again).

27 Some textures found in the coats of animals are easily interpreted into a fabric medium if colour is used. Imagine that it is not possible to use colour and that you have been commissioned to portray a bird (eg a peacock) three dimensionally, using only white and silver, for a window display showing white wedding shoes. Possible materials are pearls, silver wire and thread, nets, leather, suede, silk, rayon and white and silver beads and sequins. This requires a different approach to the study of the bird in your museum.

28 At the beginning of term make a scrapbook about museums. Include the following items that you have collected during the holiday: (a) every picture, article or advertisement that you have found in newspapers or magazines about museums; (b) information cut from the *Radio Times*

about every talk on the radio that has involved museums; (c) cuttings from the *Radio Times* and *TV Times* about every relevant programme on the television, including photographs where available. If it is difficult or impossible to obtain the cuttings, listen to or watch the programmes and take notes. Or make drawings of posters you have seen on railway stations and in the street advertising museums. You can add a report of a visit made on your own or with the school, saying what you saw, enjoyed, or didn't like. Incorporate useful information, postcards and drawings.

29   The word 'cat' can refer to the 'king of the jungle', the sacred Egyptian animal or a domestic pet. Look round your museums at the various portrayals of these. Choose two of them and write a short sketch consisting of a conversation between the two about their country, food, habits and ideas. Make large paper masks of each, giving them huge green or yellow eyes, pointed ears and exaggerated characteristics. Wear these to perform a short mime and a spoken play could follow. Try and bring out the pride, independence and other feline attributes of each type of cat.

30   Make a silhouette picture of one of the following: (a) a wart-hog, (b) a goat, (c) a squirrel, (d) a rhinoceros, (e) a beetle, (f) a flying dragon from Malaysia. Find details about their appearance in the natural history section of your museum.

31   Write a story about one of the sleigh dogs in the Artic, bringing into the story (a) an iceberg, (b) a blizzard, (c) a penguin, (d) a ship, (e) Christmas dinner, (f) a broken gramophone, (g) a torn flag. Illustrate. Discover all you can about the things mentioned by looking round museums, so that details in the story and the illustrations are as authentic as possible.

32   You have been asked to devise a new animated cartoon for a film, using three of the following animals: zebra, giraffe, kangaroo, sloth, lyre bird, or bison. Get ideas about these from your museums. Give an outline of the plot, and describe and name the chosen stars.

33   Elephants can conjure up images of rides at the zoo, circuses or methods of transport for maharajahs. Look at stuffed elephants in museums and at designs of elephants in paintings, carvings, embroideries and prints. Do some preliminary sketches and then make one of the following: (a) a machined picture, (b) a wool picture, (c) a linocut, (d) a fabric collage, (e) a painting.

34   Imagine that you are living in early Egyptian, Chinese, Greek, Roman, Indian or Mexican times, and that you have been asked to give a talk on BBC Radio's *Woman's Hour*. Pick one person to give a general introduction and choose five other people to help you, each of you to be an expert on one of the following topics: (a) housing, (b) beauty and fashion, (c) health, (d) food, (e) education, (f) the arts.

35 There is an arts festival in progress, and a large shop in your nearest town or city has agreed to put on a window display advertising a representative selection of exhibits from your local museum to encourage people to visit it during the festival. Look at all the exhibits in the museum and make notes and sketches of those you think should be included. There should be at least one item to represent each section of the museum and the sizes, shapes, textures and colours should be as varied as possible. Make a large picture of the shop window containing the display, and include an advertisement which mentions the name of the museum, where it is and times of opening.

36 Imagine that *This is your life* on Independent Television has the ability to go back years in time. Pick one of your local famous people who is featured in your museum. Find out all you can from personal relics, pictures and other exhibits and information. Fill in any gaps from your local library. Pick an interviewer and someone to represent (a) the mother or father, (b) the teacher, (c) a childhood friend, (d) an adult friend, (e) a person in the same work or profession. Now start acting.

37 Look at the following first, in the natural history section, and then in designs by various artists and craftsmen: (a) crocodile, (b) lion, (c) camel, (d) fish. Make a picture of one of them in one of the following media (beads or sequins can be added): (a) string in various widths and colours, (b) wool, (c) suede and leather, (d) coloured nets.

38 Find one of the following in your museum: (a) a Roman toy, (b) a Greek terracotta bull, (c) a Staffordshire china dog. Imagine you lived in the age when this was designed. Make up a story about where and how it was made and where you bought it. Describe the room you kept it in, and the pleasure it gave you. Paint a picture to illustrate part of the text.

39 Study animals on plates, flags, prints and textiles in your museum. Think of an animal which would have significance as a heraldic crest for you when you became the head of your family. Consider your place of birth, a favourite sport, an interest or a personal characteristic and choose an animal which seems to represent this. Sketch it so that it fits into the correct heraldic shape, then cut out in paper, stitch or paint a finished example.

40 Look round your local church. Which animals can you see in the stained glass, sculpture, or wooden or bronze decoration? Compare these with those you have seen in your museum made in the same media.

41 Find all the information you can about the subjects in your museums. Imagine you are one of the newsreaders on the radio and make up news of events from ancient (a) Rome, (b) Athens, (c) Egypt, (d) Africa, (e) China. This can be news of discovery, building, craft, dancing displays, interesting people, disaster or anything else you can think of. Some of these items can be tape-recorded by various members of the class acting different parts, and introduced by the newsreader.

42 In Borneo the stylised form of the great hornbill appears in the icons of war. This is a grotesque-looking bird, as large as a turkey and it is held in great awe by the natives of Asia – understandably so, as it has a strange barking call and alternates between a gliding flight and a furious flapping of wings, the beat of which can be heard a mile away. Paint a surrealistic picture of this bird, making it as terrifying as possible.

43 Go to one of the films shown at your museum, study it carefully and comment on the following: (a) presentation of the title (lettering, layout, drawings or photographs), (b) music (dramatic, inventive, quiet, loud, slow, fast, familiar theme), (c) colour, (if in black and white whether the contrast between tones are interesting or if the colour is good, too blue, too orange, or any other defects), (d) presentation of the story, (concise, interesting, muddled, inventive), (e) voices (whether the commentator has a lively, dull, raspish, well modulated way of talking), (f) actors, (whether professional people are taking part or amateurs or people who are neither but interested in the subject portrayed), (g) whether it is easily understood or too technical, (h) humour (if any), (i) photography. What film would you like to make for your museum? How would you produce it? How many people would take part? What aspects of the subject would it cover?

44 Imagine you are holding an exhibition in a museum showing people of importance from this century; which person from each of the following categories would you include? (a) inventor, (b) actor, (c) politician, (d) discoverer, (e) writer, (f) artist, (g) musician. First decide what objects would you choose to represent each of them. Then pick one of the following media to represent each person and say how it would be used to portray its subjects: (a) wax, (b) bronze, (c) silk-screen, (d) oil-painting, (e) wood, (f) fabric, (g) etching. There is also a huge photograph of each person. State in each case whether this would be the face only or a full-length figure and what kind of background it would have. You now have three items for each person. What fourth item would you choose for each one to complete the display? Make a colour sketch of one of these people with the four items you have chosen to represent him or her.

45 Make a list of all the objects incorporating flower designs in your museum. Describe three of them.

46 Look round your museum and find something you consider to be (a) sad, (b) amusing, (c) ugly, (d) menacing, (e) spiritual, (f) beautiful.

47 Look for some of these qualities in the natural history section: (a) pattern – the horned horizontal bands on the armadillo, the scales on fishes, the feathered shapes on birds. (b) Texture – soft matted 'wool' of a camel's coat, hard 'string' or wiry 'corded' effect of a porcupine's spines, 'suede' and 'leathered' effect of a rhinoceros' skin. (c) Colour – colouring sometimes helps to establish a rhythm, movement and pattern

for a truer rendering of an animal. Paint or embroider a picture using one of these.

48   Look out for the following when a temporary exhibition of contemporary embroidery is being shown: (a) the most original design, (b) good design but poor technique, (c) poor design but good technique. Comment in writing on the three examples, pointing out the good things and making constructive suggestions for altering any failings you may feel are reflected in the works, for instance:

Use of too many colours (cancelling each other out).

Use of too many stitches (creating a muddled ' sampler ').

Design-wise – are there too many shapes which ' balance ' each other and become dull? Or are the shapes too haphazard? Can many different textures and stitches kill the original imagery or are they likely to be more stimulating?

49   Which is your favourite museum out of all those you have visited? Why?

5 Three projects

The value of large-scale projects lies in the fact that they enable group work and individual research in such subjects as history, English geography, art and craftwork to be carried on simultaneously, rather than requiring concentration on a single subject for each lesson. Everyone can contribute: those who are good at English can write, history and geography enthusiasts can do research, those who can paint and draw can do the art work and those who are good at making models or using tools can be responsible for the craftwork.

The outlines for projects suggested here need not, of course, be followed to the letter. Some ways of adapting them for other subjects or periods are suggested at the end of this chapter.

1 ANGLO-SAXON

Plan an exhibition to be held in a museum (represented by a hall or classroom), which will be unusual, interesting and exciting, and will increase the public's knowledge about the Anglo-Saxon period or about certain aspects of life then, such as war, pottery, farming, weaving and so on. Clothes, embroidered items, models and other exhibits will be made by the children.

Appoint the following officers: a museum keeper, to direct proceedings this could be the teacher); assistant keepers, to do research and prepare material for labels; research assistants and museum assistants, to help with research, do the lettering, arrange displays, do drawings and take photographs; an education officer, to organise lectures; and an exhibition planner, to design the exhibition.

The first task is to hit upon a new and imaginative way of presenting the exhibition. This need not be complicated – a simple approach often has greater impact. You could, with the planner's approval, use one of these eye-catchers: (a) a large structure to contain the whole exhibition, eg an Anglo-Saxon hut, part of a church or a ship; (b) a huge principal motif, eg a helmet, a shield, a plough; (c) a border to go round the exhibition with an Anglo-Saxon pattern, such as the twisted rope motif found on so many objects.

Movement
(a) See whether some of the objects can be made to move on a homemade turntable; or construct some models with working parts, to present a contrast with static items.
(b) Children dressed in appropriate costumes can slowly mime a duel or demonstrate weaving. Puppets could act out a story.

Lighting
Light objects displayed in semi-darkness can convey an atmosphere of mystery or discovery. Place coloured lights over some exhibits.

Materials
The cheapest materials, such as cardboard, paper and fabrics, can create an exciting display if they are used in unusual ways: dye them, paint them, make holes in them, stick on cut-up egg boxes and milk bottle tops, fold and drape them, and so on. Perforated cardboard screens painted red or black can look most dramatic.

Displaying objects
Not everything need be placed on the obvious tables. Covered chairs, ladders and any other items with flat bases can be used, or various sized boxes can be covered, painted and stood upright with an object inside, in imitation of glass display cases.

Music
Choose or compose some appropriate music to be played on tape or performed by the musicians in the class.

Ideas for exhibits
1 Who do you think was the unknown high-ranking person or king found with the treasures in the burial ship discovered at Sutton Hoo? Make up a story about him when he was alive, referring to clothes he may have worn, food he may have eaten, people he may have met and the main events in his life from childhood to death. Make a small book with stiff covers and copy out your story as neatly as possible, drawing or painting illustrations wherever possible. Design a cover, using Letraset for the title, with a picture of the interior of the burial ship. Make it sparkle with gold and silver paint.
2 Draw a cartoon strip entitled *A Day in the Life of an Anglo-Saxon Farmer.*
3 Make a set of figures depicting a king, a warrior, a farmer and a noblewoman.
4 Make some thumb pots and apply Anglo-Saxon designs to them.
5 Make a clay model of a fight between an Anglo-Saxon warrior and a Dane.

6 Make a mask of an Anglo-Saxon warrior wearing a helmet.

7 Write some verses about King Alfred (his character, legends, wars, chronicles), copy them on to a large sheet of card for display and illustrate them.

8 Make two puppets representing King Alfred and an old cottager and write a scene for them based on the tale of the burnt cakes. Make and paint scenery and any stage props you think the story requires.

9 Make your own *Chronicle* about the Anglo-Saxon period. Paint, draw or model people, kings, architecture, wars, ships, jewellery and pottery to illustrate the text.

10 Make a papier mâché plate and decorate it with patterns based on Anglo-Saxon animal motifs.

---

2 CAPTAIN COOK

If possible this project should be undertaken in conjunction with visits to the National Maritime in London.

Imagine that you are working on one of the dozen newspapers printed in London in Georgian times and covering the most exciting events of the three voyages made by Captain Cook between 1769 and 1779. (You are not expected to write eighteenth-century English.)

Decide on the name and size of your newspaper and appoint a staff as follows: an editor, who makes the final decision as to what constitutes front-page news; assistant editors, in charge of the other pages; journalists, to write about events, places, people, costumes and food; reporters, to interview interesting personalities, eg Captain Cook, the ship's doctor, the cabin boy, a chieftain, a native girl; illustrators to sketch incidents, islands, ships and fights; photographers, to photograph people, places and events; (although the medium was not invented then it might be helped to use it for this project) and typographers, responsible for layout, lettering and print. There will also be opportunities for costume designers and makers to provide appropriate dress for the main characters, who can then be photographed in action. Artists, musicians, poets and cartoonists can join in by sending contributions to the editor. Budding playwrights can attempt a *Life and Death of Captain Cook.*

Journalists

Write about islands, natives, costumes, customs, plants, vegetables, animals, boats, battles, weapons, weather; the landing at Tahiti; the death of Captain Cook.

Reporters

Interview Captain Cook asking questions such as How long have you been at sea?, What did you do before that?, What is the name of the country you have discovered?, What kind of navigation instruments, maps and charts did you take with you?, What is the name of your ship?, What trading goods did you take for the natives?, Were they afraid of you?, How did you treat scurvy?.

Interview one of the natives: Did you think Captain Cook was a god?, Were you afraid of him?, What presents did you give him?, How did you make him understand you?

Illustrators
Draw and paint: the islands and natives; the landing and trading; the *Endeavour*; Captain Cook; animals; instruments; weapons; the death of Captain Cook; charts and maps of voyages.

Typographers
Arrange illustrations and pictures, except on the front page where the editor's word must be regarded as final. You may have to persuade the assistant editors to leave out or insert certain things to achieve a professional-looking result.

You may also like to include the following:

Women's page
Fashions, food, women's point of view, social column.

Children's page
Native toys, native children's poems, ideas and games.

---

3 FOUR GEORGIAN KINGS

There is a tendency to lose sight of the fact that the Georgian period covered over a hundred years, from 1714 to 1830, and that during that time many changes took place. Some of these can be demonstrated in the course of this project.

Imagine that you are planning a series of four one-act plays for television, in correct costumes and settings. Each play is to be based on a discussion between one of the kings and a famous person of the time which takes place in a room in Bath, Brighton or London.

The following people will be required for programme planning: a producer (possibly the teacher), scriptwriters, designers and researchers. All suggestions will be discussed by the producer and the scriptwriters, studied in depth by the researchers and sketched by the designers. Cover all aspects of the following topics throughout the four reigns which are known collectively as the Georgian period: (a) costume, (b) social history, (c) architecture, (d) invention, (e) furniture, (f) pictures and wall decorations, (g) *objets d'art*.

G

The aim of the project is to produce the following: (a) an original play with four short scenes, one for each of the four Georges; (b) paintings, drawings, collages and models; (c) designs for costumes with suggestions for materials and colours; (d) designs for furniture, wall decorations, carpets and ornaments; (e) scenery for the play in the form of a large painted window showing the landscape outside the room and some glimpses of external architecture.

Notes on the Georgian period

WOMEN'S COSTUME

George I   Narrow skirts, tight sleeves cut to elbow length, bustled overskirts, high lace caps.

George II   Bustles reduced to panniers, added trains, Dolly Varden hats.

George III   Balloon skirts, later split, high white wigs replace hats, overskirts and trains become bustles, necks covered with full fichus, Empire women in thinned-down Greek styles.

George IV   Flared skirts and sleeves, feathered top hats.

MEN'S COSTUME

George I   Tight coats (bottom half unbuttoned), stiff wigs, squared hats.

George II   Disclosed waistcoats, flared coat skirts, shortened wigs, three-cornered hats.

George III   Shorter waistcoats, tighter wigs.

George IV   Lower front of coat removed, revers added, stand-up collars, top boots.

TRANSPORT

Sedan-chairs, covered coaches, open-sided back-to-back carts, open inward-facing pony carts, private carriages with exaggerated wheels, hackney coaches.

ARCHITECTURE

Early Georgian   More academic, less free; exteriors quiet but somewhat heavy and massive; extensive use of decoration, interiors often rich and florid.

Late Georgian   Very refined, reflecting Greek and late Roman styles; modelling very delicate, sometimes over-thin; Greek-influenced interiors with delicate plaster decoration.

FURNITURE

Sheraton   Rectangular shapes, straight lines, inlay and carving, chairs, dressing-tables, inlaid satinwood kneehole desks.

Chippendale   Gothic, French and Chinese influenced chairs, often made of mahogany with cabriole legs.

Hepplewhite Marquetry, Chinese-style lacquer chairs, shield- or heart-shaped chairbacks, bookcases.
Adam Marble fireplaces with figures.

POTTERY
Wedgwood New cream-coloured porcelain, 'queen's ware', and pale blue unglazed porcelain, 'jasper ware'.
Chelsea pottery Scent bottles, figures, animals.

GLASS
1745 Jacobite wine-glasses with a rosebud symbolising the Young Pretender. Stems decorated with colourful, twisted designs. Waterford cut-glass from Ireland.

SILVER
Sauceboats, sugar tongs, sweetmeat baskets, plated tea-caddies, inkstands, coffee pots, salvers. Silver marks often included portraits of George III and IV.

PAINTINGS
George Stubbs Horses, carriages, people in the costume of the period.
William Hogarth Portraits and social life of the Georgian period.
Joseph Turner Magnificent landscapes and seascapes.
Thomas Gainsborough Portraits and landscapes.
John Constable Landscapes.

GEORGIAN KINGS
George I   1714–1727
George II   1727–1760
George III 1760–1820
George IV   1820–1830

SUGGESTIONS FOR THE KING'S VISITORS IN PROJECT 3
Naval commander Horatio, Viscount Nelson
Explorer Captain James Cook
Artists William Hogarth, Sir Joshua Reynolds, Joseph Turner, Thomas Gainsborough, William Blake, John Constable
Writers Dr Samuel Johnson, Samuel Taylor Coleridge, Sir Walter Scott, William Wordsworth, Jane Austen, Percy Bysshe Shelley, Lord Byron, John Keats
Musicians George Frederick Handel, Wolfgang Amadeus Mozart
Craftsmen Robert Adam, Thomas Chippendale, George Hepplewhite, Thomas Sheraton, Josiah Wedgwood
Architects William Kent, Robert Adam

Inventors   James Watt, Alois Senefelder, George Stephenson, Sir Richard Arkwright

Statesmen   Charles James Fox, Sir Robert Walpole, William Pitt the Elder, William Pitt the Younger.

Suggestions for adapting the three projects for different subjects

1   Anglo-Saxon

This is suitable for straightforward adaptation for any period in history and requires no elaboration.

2   Captain Cook

Substitute dramatic events from the life of any famous man or woman. The following interviews are possibilities: (a) Florence Nightingale, after her first day's experience of nursing soldiers wounded in the Crimean War; (b) William Shakespeare, after watching the first performance of one of his plays; (c) Sir Francis Drake, after the defeat of the Spanish Armada; (d) Anna Pavlova after her first performance of the leading role in *Swan Lake*; (e) George Stephenson, after the first journey of the *Rocket*; (f) Napoleon or Wellington after the Battle of Waterloo.

There are many small museums devoted to a local or national figure who could be the subject of project 2. Here are some examples:

Jane Austen   Alton, Chawton, Hampshire

Thomas Carlyle   The Arched House, Ecclefechan, Dumfriesshire

John Ruskin   Ruskin Museum, Coniston, Lancashire

Ellen Terry   Smallhythe, near Tenterden, Kent.

3   Four Georgian Kings

Any four monarchs, not necessarily from consecutive periods, could be the subjects for project 3, provided that each scene is in period.

6 Museums in the British Isles

Existing museum services and loans are marked under the names and addresses of the museums concerned as follows:
* services; loans to county, city, town or area
Δ services only.
Most large museums will arrange lectures if given adequate notice.

Services may include:
Lectures, the museum's own live or recorded television programmes, guided tours, films, slides, discussions, trying on period clothes, touching or working chosen objects, and listening to music and readings from a chosen period. Also workrooms and studios with supplies of books, visual aids, painting, drawing and craft materials. Quiz sheets. Children's clubs. Holiday activities.

Circulation and loan collections may include:
Films and slides; books; oil-paintings, collages, watercolours, linocuts, etchings, drawings and reproductions; pottery, weaving and embroidery; natural history models, geological and botanical specimens.
Lists of loans available are sometimes issued on request and can always be consulted at the museum. Special requirements will be met if practicable.

ENGLAND

BEDFORDSHIRE
Bedford
Bedford Museum, The Embankment   Tel Bedford 53323   Local antiquities, history, industries and natural history. Coins, maps, prints, including Bedford modern school collections. *The Bunyan Collection, Public Library, Harpur Street   Tel Bedford 50931*   John Bunyan, life and works.
The Bunyan Meeting Library and Museum, Mill Street   Personal relics and works. *Cecil Higgins Art Gallery, Castle Close   Tel Bedford 53791*   Furniture, glass, porcelain, silver, embroidery. Watercolours and prints.

Elstow

Elstow Moot Hall   *Tel Bedford 66889*   John Bunyan collection.

Luton

Luton Museum and Art Gallery, Wardown Park   *Tel Luton 21725*
Local archaeology, history, trades, crafts, furniture, woodwork, decorative
and fine art. Costume, needlework, dolls and toys. *Apply to Education
Service Officer.*

BERKSHIRE

Abingdon

Borough Museum, The County Hall   *Tel Abingdon 3703*   Local
archaeology, fossils, history. Costumes, uniforms, toys.
The Guildhall   *Tel Abingdon 851*   Historic corporation silver and
plate. Paintings.
*Pendon Museum of Miniature Landscape and Transport, Long
Wittenham*   *Tel Clifton Hampden 365*   Railway relics. Miniature
scenes of countryside and transport.

Maidenhead

Harry Reitlinger Bequest, Oldfield, Riverside   *Tel Maidenhead 21818*
Chinese, European, Italian, Persian pottery. Sculpture, glass, paintings
and drawings.

Newbury

Borough Museum, Wharf Street   *Tel Newbury 4000*   Local
archaeology, geology, history and natural history.

Reading

Museum and Art Gallery, Blagrave Street   *Tel Reading 55911*   Local
archaeology, natural history, prehistoric and medieval metalwork. Delft
collection. Changing art exhibitions. *Apply to Schools Liaison Officer,*
Schools Service Section, 28 Castle Street, Reading. Competitions.
Museum of English Rural Life, Whiteknights Park   *Tel Reading
85123*   Country living including agriculture, farm implements, tools,
crafts, utensils.
Museum of Greek Archaeology, Whiteknights Park   Greek and
Egyptian antiquities.

Windsor

The Guildhall Exhibitions, High Street   *Tel Windsor 66167*   Local
history, natural history. Royal portraits, dioramas.

BUCKINGHAMSHIRE

Aylesbury
Buckinghamshire County Museum, 9 Church Street Tel Aylesbury 82158 County archaeology, natural history, history, local crafts, costume and silver, paintings. Loan exhibitions. *Apply to Schools' Museum Assistant.*

Chalfont St Giles
Milton's Cottage Tel Chalfont St Giles 2313 Relics, portraits, busts, local objects and maps.

Eton
Eton College Natural History Museum British birds, ethnological and entomological specimens, mammals, reptiles, fossils.

High Wycombe
Art Gallery and Museum, Castle Hill Tel High Wycombe 23879 Chairs, tools, lace and local items.

Olney
Cowper and Newton Museum, Market Place Tel Olney 516 Belongings, manuscripts and local items.

Waddesdon
Waddesdon Manor Eighteenth-century furniture, carpets, Sèvres porcelain, small arms. Aviary. Paintings.

Winslow
Florence Nightingale Museum, Claydon House, Claydon Tel Steeple Claydon 349 Paintings and objects.

CAMBRIDGESHIRE

Cambridge
Cambridge and County Folk Museum, 2–3 Castle Street Tel Cambridge 55159 Local history, agriculture and trade exhibits. Toys, pictures.
Fitzwilliam Museum, Trumpington Street Tel Cambridge 50023 Egyptian and W. Asiatic antiquities. Ceramics, textiles, coins. Paintings.
The Scott Polar Research Institute, Lensfield Road Tel Cambridge 55601 Scientific work, relics, equipment from expeditions. Eskimo art.
Sedgwick Museum of Geology, Downing Street Tel Cambridge 51585 Fossils, rocks, stones and marbles.

University Museum of Archaeology and Ethnology, Downing Street
Tel Cambridge 59714 Prehistoric to medieval archaeology from several countries. Ethnographical material from America, Africa and Oceania.
University Museum of Classical Archaeology, Little St Mary's Lane
Tel Cambridge 52410 Casts of Greek and Roman sculpture.
University Museum of Mineralogy and Petrology, Downing Street
Tel Cambridge 64131 Minerals and rocks.
University Museum of Zoology and Comparative Anatomy, Downing Street Zoological specimens.
Whipple Museum of the History of Science, Free School Lane
Tel Cambridge 50329 Historic scientific instruments.
Δ *Apply to the Museum Teacher, County Museum Service, 9 Castle Street, Cambridge. *Apply to Museum Loan Service, Teachers' Centre, Back Hill, Ely.*

Wisbech
Wisbech and Fenland Museum, Museum Square Natural history, pottery, porcelain. Archaeological and antiquarian collections. Books and manuscripts.

CHANNEL ISLANDS

Guernsey, St Peter Port
Castle Cornet Tel Guernsey 21657 Military and Maritime Museum, ship models, thread pictures, photographs and paintings.
Guille Alles Museum Tel Guernsey 20392 German occupation. Natural history, farming.
Hauteville House, 38 Hauteville Tel Guernsey 21911 Victor Hugo's house. Relics, china, furniture, tapestries.
Lukis and Island Museum, St Barnabas, Cornet Street Channel Islands archaeology and anthropology. Chinese porcelain. Works of art.

Jersey, St Helier
Gorey Castle Museum, Gorey Pottery, coins, glass, clay pipes. Regimental buttons.

CHESHIRE

Altrincham
Art Gallery and Museum, George Street Tel Altrincham 0317 Local history. Art collection. Loan collections.

Birkenhead
Williamson Art Gallery and Museum, Slatey Road Tel Birkenhead

4177 Shipping gallery. Ceramics. English watercolours and oil paintings. Art exhibitions.

Bramhall
Bramall Hall Portraits, tapestries, murals.

Chester
Grosvenor Museum, Grosvenor Street Tel Chester 21616 Anglo-Saxon coins, Roman antiquities, sculptured stones. Natural and local history.
King Charles's Tower, City Walls Dioramas and exhibits illustrating Civil War.
Water Tower, City Walls Chester in the Middle Ages. Dioramas and exhibits.

Macclesfield
Museum and Art Gallery, Prestbury Road Tel Macclesfield 24067 Egyptian antiquities. Local exhibitions. Victorian paintings.

Port Sunlight
The Lady Lever Art Gallery Tel Port Sunlight 3623 Chinese pottery and porcelain. Wedgwood china. Carved stones and crystals. English furniture. Sculpture, paintings, miniatures.

Runcorn
The Shaw Museum, Cross Street Pictures and photographs of Runcorn. Excavated historical objects.

Stalybridge
The Astley Cheetham Art Gallery, Trinity Street Tel Stalybridge 2708 Egyptian, Greek and Roman antiquities. Local history, geology, natural history. Art collection. Changing exhibitions.

Stockport
Municipal Museum, Vernon Park, Turncraft Lane Tel Stockport 3668 Local history, natural history, geology, ceramics. Victoriana. Temporary exhibitions.

CORNWALL

Bodmin
Passmore Edwards Public Library and Museum, Lower Bore Street Local history collection.

Camborne

Camborne School of Metalliferous Mining Museum   Tel Camborne 2167   Minerals and ores. Robert Hunt memorial museum.

Public Library and Museum, Cross Street   Archaeology, mineralogy, local history and antiquities.

Harlyn Bay

Harlyn Bay Prehistoric Burial Ground and Museum, near Padstow Tel St Merryn 335   Prehistoric remains, jewellery, skulls, urns, implements.

Helston

Helston Borough Museum, Old Butter Market   Folk museum. Local life. Early wireless section.

Looe

The Cornish Museum, Lower Street, East Looe   Tel Liskeard 2423   Life and culture of Cornwall. Folklore. Relics (witchcraft, charms), arts, crafts, fishing, games.

Penzance

Penzance History and Antiquarian Museum, Penlee Park   Tel Penzance 2345/3954   Archaeological, antiquarian and tin mining exhibits. Relics, local history.

Tresco (Isles of Scilly)

Valhalla Maritime Museum, Tresco Abbey   Tel Scillionia 876   Figureheads and ships' ornaments from wrecks off the Isles of Scilly.

Truro

County Museum and Art Gallery, River Street   Tel Truro 2205   Local antiquities and history. Japanese ivories and lacquer. Pewter, pottery, porcelain, minerals, paintings.

Zennor

Wayside Museum, Old Millhouse   West Cornwall archaeology. Folk collections, domestic, agriculture, and mining exhibits.

CUMBERLAND

Carlisle

Museum and Art Gallery, Tullie House, Castle Street   Tel Carlisle 24166   Prehistoric and Roman remains. Birds, mammals, geology. Porcelain and pre-Raphaelite paintings.

Keswick
Fitzpark Museum and Art Gallery, Station Road   Local geology,
natural history. Manuscripts by writers and poets.

DERBYSHIRE

Bakewell
The Old House Museum, Cunningham Place   Tel Bakewell 2918   Folk
and industrial archaeology collection.

Birchover
The Heathcote Museum, near Matlock   Tel Winster 313
Archaeological finds from local Middle Bronze Age sites.

Buxton
Buxton Museum, Terrace Road   Tel Buxton 4658   Local history and
geology. Ashford marble and Blue John ornaments. Paintings, prints,
pottery, glass.

Chesterfield
Revolution House, Old Whittington   Tel Chesterfield 2047/2661   Inn
connected with 1688 revolution plot. Seventeenth-century furniture.

Crich
The Tramway Museum, near Matlock   Horse, steam, electric tramcars.

Derby
Derby Museum and Art Gallery, Strand   Local archaeology, natural
history and history. Porcelain pictures by Joseph Wright of Derby. *For
services, apply to Schools Liaison Officer. For loans, apply to Derbyshire
Museum Organiser, Park Grange, Duffield Road, Derby.*

DEVON

Ashburton
Ashburton Museum, 1 West Street   Local antiquities, costumes,
weapons, implements. American Indian antiques.

Barnstaple
The North Devon Athenaeum, The Square   Tel Barnstaple 2174
Local antiquities, cryptograms, geological exhibits.
St Anne's Chapel Museum, St Peter's Churchyard, High Street   Local
interest exhibits. Prints, drawings, pottery, seals, firearms.

Bideford

Bideford Museum, Municipal Buildings   Tel Bideford 486   North Devon pottery. Geological specimens, shipwright's tools, prints.

Brixham

Brixham Museum, Higher Street   Local geology, archaeology and history. Maritime folk museum.

Exeter

Royal Albert Memorial Museum and Art Gallery, Queen Street Tel Exeter 56724   Natural history, ethnography, costume, silver, ceramics, glass. Paintings, watercolours (Devon artists), temporary exhibitions.

Honiton

Honiton and Allhallows Public Museum, High Street   Tel Honiton 2921 Local collection, lace, implements and Devon kitchen. Straight-tusked elephant, hippopotamus bones, red deer, all 100 000 years old. Relics of first and second world wars.

Ilfracombe

Ilfracombe Museum, Wilder Road   Tel Ilfracombe 3541   North Devon birds, mammals, reptiles and insects. British botany collections. Marine life and arms. Paintings and engravings.

Morwellham

Morwellham Quay Museum, near Tavistock   Tel Gunnislake 766 Industrial archaeology. Natural history. Copper port of nineteenth century, quays and water wheels.

Plymouth

Buckland Abbey, near Yelverton   Tel Yelverton 3607   Sir Francis Drake's home. Folk gallery, relics, model ships.
City Museum and Art Gallery, Tavistock Road   Tel Plymouth 6800 Archaeology, natural history. Porcelain, silver. Model ships. Paintings and drawings. *Apply to Schools Service Assistant.*
Elizabethan House, 32 New Street   Sixteenth-century house with period furnishings.

Sidmouth

Sidmouth Museum, Woolcombe House, Woolcombe Lane   Medieval hall, museum objects.

South Molton

South Molton Museum, Town Hall, Guildhall   Agricultural and historical exhibits. Eighteenth-century fire-engine, weights and measures, wig-making tools, stocks, man-traps. Pewter.

Torquay
Torquay Natural History Society Museum, Babbacombe Road Tel Torquay 23975 Local folk culture, natural history, caves. *Apply to Schools Museum Officer.*
Torre Abbey Art Gallery, Abbey Gardens Tel Torquay 23593 Furniture, monastic ruins, pictures, prints and miniatures.

Totnes
The Elizabethan House, 70 Fore Street Tel Totnes 3532 Archaeological exhibits, tools, domestic articles, toys. Period furniture and costumes.

DORSET

Bridport
Bridport Museum and Art Gallery, South Street Tel Bridport 2166 Local antiquities, natural history and agriculture. Paintings and drawings.

Dorchester
Dorset County Museum, High West Street Tel Dorchester 2735 Dorset geology, natural history, history. Thomas Hardy memorial room. Pictures and prints by Dorset artists.

Lyme Regis
The Philpot Museum, Bridge Street Tel Lyme Regis 3127 Local geology, history, prints, coins. Fire engine of 1710.

Poole
Old Town House, High Street Tel Poole 6066 Local history, pottery, china, ships, shipping. Dug-out canoe from Bronze Age.
Poole Museum, South Road Local antiquities, fauna (sea-birds), history (including pottery, trade tokens, weapons and armour). Maritime history.

Portland
Portland Island Museum, Avice's Cottage, Wakeham Local historical folk collection and natural history.

Shaftesbury
Abbey Ruins Museum, Park Walk Tel Shaftesbury 2910 Carved stones, medieval tiles. Models of church and town before 1539.

Local History Museum, Gold Hill   Tel Shaftesbury 2157   Button collection. Local archaeology, tools, crafts and Victoriana. Fire-engine of 1744.

Sherborne
Sherborne Museum, Abbey Gate House   Tel Sherborne 2252   Local geology, history, model castles and Victorian dolls' house.

Wimborne Minster
Priest's House Museum, High Street   Local archaeology, history. Tudor building with garden.

COUNTY DURHAM

Barnard Castle
The Bowes Museum   Tel Barnard Castle 2139   Period settings, pottery, jewellery, tapestries, glass. Paintings, sculpture, metalwork. Toys. *Apply to the Schools Museum Officer.*

Darlington
Darlington Museum, Tubwell Row   Tel Darlington 2034   Local and natural history, machinery and model engines.

Durham
Gulbenkian Museum of Oriental Art and Archaeology, Elvet Hill Tel Durham 66711   Egyptian and Mesopotamian antiquities. Chinese pottery, porcelain, paintings and textiles. Indian sculpture. Japanese and Tibetan Art. Temporary exhibitions.

Gateshead
Saltwell Park Museum, Saltwell Park   Tel Gateshead 72811   Local natural history, pottery, glass, prints, wood carving, dolls.

Hartlepool
Gray Art Gallery and Museum, Clarence Road   Tel Hartlepool 68916 Local industries. Chinese porcelain. Indian idols. British birds. Pictures. Loan exhibitions.

Middlesbrough, Teeside
Dorman Museum, Linthorpe Road   Tel Middlesbrough 83781 Regional archaeology, geology, natural history. Model ships. Paintings. Changing exhibitions. *Apply to Schools Service Organiser.*

Redcar, Teeside
Redcar Museum of Fishing and Shipping   Local industrial history. Ship models and oldest lifeboat.

South Shields
Roman Fort and Museum, Baring Street   Tel South Shields 61396
Roman antiquities. Stones, enamels, pottery, seals and sword.
South Shields Museum, Ocean Road   Tel South Shields 4321   Natural history, local glass, ship models and lifeboats.

Stockton, Teeside
Preston Hall Museum, Preston Park, Eaglescliffe   Local pottery, arms, toys. Period rooms.
Stockton and Darlington Railway Museum   Tel Stockton 62803
Historic pictures and relics.

Sunderland
Museum and Art Gallery, Borough Road   Tel Sunderland 70417-8
Archaeology, botany, geology, zoology, natural history. Pottery, silver. Model ships. Paintings, sculpture. Loan exhibitions.

ESSEX

Chelmsford
Chelmsford and Essex Museum, Oaklands Park   Tel Chelmsford 60614 (Mon–Fri) 53006 (weekend)   Regional antiquities, coins, costumes. British birds. Paintings.

Colchester
Colchester and Essex Museum
1   *The Castle   Tel Colchester 7745*   Local history, Roman jewellery, pottery, glass, bronzes. *Apply to Schools Officer.*
2   *Hollytrees*   Georgian house. Local history and costume.
3   *Natural History Museum, All Saint's Church, High Street*
Tel Colchester 73669   Diorama. Regional natural history.
The Minories, High Street   Georgian furniture, china. Modern and past art loan exhibitions.

Grays
Thurrock Local History Museum, Central Library, Orsett Road
Tel Thurrock 76827   Archaeology. Local agriculture, social and industrial history.

Ingatestone
Ingatestone Hall   Tel Ingatestone 3340   Documents, prints. Furniture, armorial china. Sixteenth-century virginal.

Saffron Walden
Saffron Walden Museum, Museum Street   Tel Saffron Walden 2494
Local archaeology, geology, natural history, ethnology. Ceramics and glass.

Southend-on-Sea
Prittlewell Priory Museum, 4 Priory Park   Tel Southend-on-Sea 42878
Regional archaeology, history, social life and natural history.

GLOUCESTERSHIRE

Bristol
Blaise Castle House Museum, Henbury   Tel Bristol 625378   Objects from former English life. Folk park exhibits (cornmill and dairy).
Bristol City Art Gallery and Museum, Queen's Road   Tel Bristol 25908
See chapter 3.
Red Lodge, Park Row   Tel Bristol 21903   Elizabethan house. Furnishings.

Broadway
Snowshill Manor   Tel Broadway 2410   Musical instruments, clocks, bicycles, toys.

Chedworth
Chedworth Villa   Tel Withington 256   One of the best-preserved Roman villas with mosaic pavements and site finds.

Cheltenham
Cheltenham Art Gallery and Museum, Clarence Street   Tel Cheltenham 22476   Local archaeology, geology, natural history. Furnished rooms, pottery, porcelain. Paintings. *Apply to Assistant Curator and Schools Museum Officer.*

Cirencester
Corinium Museum, Park Street   Tel Cirencester 2248   Local antiquities. Roman sculpture, mosaic and domestic items.

Filkins
Filkins and Broughton Poggs Museum, near Lechlade   Local folklore, tools, domestic items.

Children attending classes at the Victoria and Albert Museum, London

Harrison's First Marine Timekeeper 1737 and Kendall's watches. *Left* K2 carried by Bligh on his last voyage. *Centre* Prize-winning watch No 4 1759. *Right* K1 carried by Cook and Vancouver
National Maritime Museum, on loan from Ministry of Defence (Navy)

Gloucester
*Bishop Hooper's Lodging, 99–103 Westgate Street   Tel Gloucester
.24131*   Regional crafts and industries. Local history and history of the
Gloucestershire Regiment.
City Museum and Art Gallery, Brunswick Road   Tel Gloucester 24131
Local archaeology, geology, natural history, pottery, silver, glass, costume
and furniture. Temporary art exhibitions.

Stroud
Stroud Museum, Lansdown   Tel Stroud 3394   Archaeology, geology,
local crafts, farming equipment, ceramics, dolls, pictures.

Winchcombe
Folk Museum, Town Hall   Objects of local interest.

HAMPSHIRE

Alton
Curtis Museum, High Street   Tel Alton 82802   Folk collection, local
natural history and archaeology, geology. Pottery, porcelain, glass.

Basingstoke
Willis Museum, New Street   Tel Basingstoke 65902   Local archaeology
geology, horology. Costume, textiles, watchmakers' tools, clocks.
Temporary art exhibitions.

Beaulieu
Maritime Museum, Bucklers Hard   Tel Bucklers Hard 203   Model
ships. Nelson's baby-clothes. Paintings.
Montague Motor Museum, Palace Place   Tel Beaulieu 374   Veteran,
vintage and modern cycles, motor cycles and cars.

Bournemouth
*Natural Science Society's Museum, 39 Christchurch Road
Tel Bournemouth 23525*   Local archaeology and natural history. Fossils.
Rothesay Museum, 8 Bath Road   Tel Bournemouth 21009   Sixteenth-
and seventeenth-century furniture. Ceramics, shells, coins. Moths and
butterflies. Arms, armour. Model ships. Paintings.
*Russell-Cotes Art Gallery and Museum, East Cliff   Tel Bournemouth
21009*   Ceramics, miniatures, sculpture, paintings.

Christchurch
Red House Museum and Art Gallery, Quay Road   Tel Christchurch
H

2860   Regional archaeology, geology, natural history. Costumes, children's toys. Changing art exhibitions.

Portsmouth
Dickens' Birthplace Museum, 393 Commercial Road, Mile End Tel Portsmouth 26155   Charles Dickens' birthplace in 1812. Portraits, prints, letters and personal items.
Victory Museum, HM Dockyard   Tel Portsmouth 22351   Nelson relics. Panorama of Trafalgar. Figureheads, model ships, marine paintings. *Apply to Schools Service Officer, City of Portsmouth Museums,* Alexandra Road, Portsmouth.

Silchester
Calleva Museum, Rectory Grounds   Tel Silchester 322   Archaeology. Models. Seed collection.

Southampton
Bargate Guildhall Museum, High Street   Tel Southampton 22544
Local history. Changing exhibitions.
God's House Tower Museum, Town Quay   Tel Southampton 20007
Local archaeology. Pottery.
Maritime Museum, Wool House, Bugle Street   Tel Southampton 23941
Fourteenth-century wool-store. Shipping.
Tudor House Museum, St Michael's Square   Tel Southampton 24216
Period furniture, glass, costume, maritime exhibits, paintings.

Southsea
Cumberland House Museum and Art Gallery, Eastern Parade, Southsea
Furniture. Natural history.
Southsea Castle, Clarence Esplanade   Archaeology. Local and military history.

Winchester
Westgate Museum, High Street   Tel Winchester 3361   Civic history exhibits. Weights and measures.
Winchester City Museum, The Square   Tel Owlesbury 213   Regional archaeology.
Winchester College Museum   Greek pottery. Watercolours.

HEREFORDSHIRE

Hereford
Churchill Gardens Museum, Venn's Lane   Tel Hereford 67409
Costume, furniture, jewellery, paintings.

City Museum and Art Gallery, Broad Street   Tel Hereford 2456
Archaeology, geology, natural history. Silver, pottery, embroidery,
textiles, costume, toys. Pictures by local artists.
The Old House, High Town   Tel Hereford 2456   Jacobean period
museum. Furniture and objects.

HERTFORDSHIRE

Ashwell
Village Museum, Swan Street   Folk museum. Prehistoric times to
present day. Pottery, tools, tokens.

Bishop's Stortford
Rhodes Memorial Museum   Tel Bishop's Stortford 51746   Cecil
Rhodes's possessions. Historical illustrations of South and Central Africa.

Hertford
Hertford Museum, 18 Bull Plain   Tel Hertford 2686   Local
archaeology, geology, natural history. Japanese armour. Turkish swords.

Hitchin
Hitchin Museum, Raynes Park   Tel Hitchin 4476   Archaeology,
natural history. Costume. Special exhibitions.

Letchworth
*Letchworth Museum and Art Gallery, Town Square   Tel Letchworth
5647*   Regional archaeology, natural history, history. Changing art
exhibitions. *Apply to Schools Services Officer.*

St Albans
City Museum, Hatfield Road   Tel St Albans 56679   County
archaeology, geology and natural history. Glass, pottery, tools. Local
trades.
Clock Tower, Market Place   Medieval pottery, glass. Historical prints.
Verulamium Museum, St Michael's   Tel St Albans 54659/59919
Mosaics. Material from Roman and Belgic cities. *Apply to Schools
Officer.*

Stevenage
Stevenage, Lytton Way, New Town Centre   Tel Stevenage 54292
Local archaeology, history and natural history. Live animals.

Tring
Zoological Museum, British Museum (Natural History), Akeman Street
Butterflies, animal specimens, shells, birds' eggs.

Watford
Watford Art Collection, Central Public Library, Hempstead Road
Tel Watford 26239/26230   Fossils, flints, pictures.

HUNTINGDONSHIRE

Huntingdon
Cromwell Museum, Market Square   Tel Huntingdon 52861
Cromwelliana, documents, portraits.

St Ives
Norris Library and Museum, The Broadway   Tel St Ives 5582   County
collections, including pottery and fen skates.

ISLE OF MAN

Castletown
Nautical Museum, Bridge Street   Schooner-rigged yacht. Deep-sea
vessel models, local fishing boats. Sailmaker's loft.

Cregneash
Manx Village Folk Museum   Furnished crofter, fisherman's cottage,
weaver's shed, turner's shop, smithy and farm.

Douglas
The Manx Museum   Tel Douglas 5522   Manx archaeology, folk life,
and natural history. Reconstructed nineteenth-century dairy, barn and
farmhouse. Manx paintings.

Port Erin
Marine Biological Museum   Marine biology research. Local fishes and
invertebrates in the aquarium. Fish hatchery.

ISLE OF WIGHT

Arreton
Arreton Manor   Tel Arreton 255   Jacobean and Elizabethan furniture.
Folk items, dolls and toys.

Brading
Osborn-Smith's Wax Museum   Tel Brading 286   Wax figures with
period costume, furniture and settings, with sound, light and motion.
The Roman Villa, Morton   Tel Brading 235   Mosaics, hypocaust and
Roman objects.

Cowes
Gilchrist Collection, The Parade Glass section including ships, walking sticks and frogs. Flags, medals, musical boxes, dolls, toys, Queen Victoria's carriage.

Newport
Carisbrooke Castle Museum Tel Newport 2107 Regional history. Charles I relics. Oldest organ in country, in playing order.

Sandown
Museum of Geology, High Street Tel Sandown 2748 Over 5,000 local fossils. Diagrams, maps, models.

KENT
Birchington
Powell-Cotton Museum, Quex Park Tel Birchington 42168 Two dioramas (African and Indian animals). Zoological specimens, native arts, crafts and objects.

Canterbury
Royal Museum, Beaney Institute, High Street Tel Canterbury 63608 Local archaeology, natural history, minerals. China, glass, jewellery, silver, pictures.
Westgate Museum Arms and armour.

Dartford
Borough Museum, Market Street Tel Dartford 21133–4 Local archaeology and geology, history, natural history, industries.

Deal
Deal Museum, Town Hall, High Street Tel Deal 4963 Local prehistoric and historic antiquities.

Dover
Dover Corporation Museum, Ladywell Tel Dover 1066 Dioramas, archaeology and natural history. Furniture, pottery, glass and embroidery.

Folkestone
Museum and Art Gallery, Grace Hill Tel Folkestone 55221
Archaeology, local history, natural science. Temporary loan exhibitions.

Herne Bay
Herne Bay Museum, High Street Tel Herne Bay 4896 Regional

exhibits, Stone, Bronze, and Iron Age. Reculver Roman material. Pictures. Maps.

Hythe
Borough Museum, Oaklands, Stade Street   Tel Hythe 6711   Local antiquities.

Maidstone
Museum and Art Gallery, St Faith's Street   Tel Maidstone 24497 Local archaeology and natural history. Ceramics, costumes, Pacific and Oriental section, paintings.

Margate
Margate Museum, Public Library, Victoria Road   Tel Thanet 23626 Local items. Saxon, Roman and other antiquities.

Richborough
Richborough Castle   Tel Sandwich 2013   Roman pottery collection, bronze ornaments, lamps, coins.

Rochester
Public Museum, Eastgate House   Tel Medway 44176   Archaeology, local history and natural history. Costumes, clocks, model ships and seaplanes. Charles Dickens relics.

Sandwich
The Guildhall Museum   Ancient items and objects of interest.

Tunbridge Wells
Royal Tunbridge Wells Museum and Art Gallery, Civic Centre Tel Tunbridge Wells 26121   Geology, natural history, toys, coins, domestic and agricultural items. Victorian paintings.

LANCASHIRE

Accrington
Haworth Art Gallery, Haworth Park   Tel Accrington 33782   Tiffany glass. English watercolours. Special exhibitions.

Bacup
Natural History Society's Museum, 24 Yorkshire Street   Local geology, domestic and natural history collections.

Barrow-in-Furness
Barrow-in-Furness Museum, Ramsden Square   Tel Barrow-in-Furness
20650   Furness area items. Finds from prehistoric sites. Model ships.

Blackburn
Museum and Art Gallery, Library Street   Tel Blackburn 59511   Local
geology, and archaeology (Egyptian). Coins, porcelain, pottery, glass and
primitive weapons. Japanese prints and other art exhibits.

Bolton
Museum and Art Gallery, Civic Centre   Tel Bolton 22311   Botany,
geology, zoology, Egyptian collection, pottery. Aquarium. Paintings and
sculpture.

Bootle
Museum and Art Gallery, Oriel Road   Tel Bootle 4040   English figure
pottery and Liverpool pottery. Art exhibitions changed monthly.

Burnley
Towneley Hall Art Gallery and Museum, Towneley Hall   Tel Burnley
24213   Archaeology, geology and natural history. Furniture, glass,
ivories, Chinese pottery, paintings.

Bury
Art Gallery and Museum, Moss Street   Tel Bury 4140   Local history,
including Bronze Age items. Paintings and sculpture.

Chorley
Astley Hall Art Gallery and Museum, Astley Park   Tel Chorley 2166
Furniture, pottery, glass, tapestries and pictures.

Clayton-le-Moors
Mercer Museum and Art Gallery, Mercer Park, Rishton Road
Tel Clayton-le-Moors 37790   John Mercer relics. Coal and coke
product collections, sea shells, and pictures.

Colne
British in India Museum, Sun Street   Dioramas, model railway, coins,
medals and stamps. Paintings.
The Colne Museum, Public Library   Local geology, natural history and
historical displays.

Coniston
The Ruskin Museum, The Institute   Tel Coniston 359   Mineral

collection. Ruskin relics. Local history, scenery and industries. Donald Campbell memorial.

Eccles
Monks Hall Museum, 42 Wellington Road   Tel Eccles 4372   Nasmyth machine tools. Pottery and historic transistors. Temporary (including art) exhibitions.

Lancaster
City Museum, Old Town Hall, Market Square   Tel Lancaster 64637 Archaeology and history. Museum of the King's Own Royal (Lancaster) Regiment. Pictures.

Leigh
Pennington Hall Museum and Art Gallery, Pennington Hall   Natural history, old machinery, silk industry. Watercolours.

Liverpool
City Museum, William Brown Street   Tel 051 207 0001   See chapter 3.
Sudley Art Gallery and Museum, Mosley Hill Road   Costume and pottery exhibits. Eighteenth- and nineteenth-century paintings.

Manchester
The Athenaeum Annexe, 81 Princess Street   Ceramics. Temporary exhibition room. ∆ *Apply to Teacher-in-charge.*
City Art Gallery, Mosley Street   Tel 061 236 2391–2   Glass, porcelain and silver. Paintings and sculpture. Frequent exhibitions.
Gallery of English Costume, Platt Hall, Rusholme   Tel 061 224 5217 Seventeenth-century costume to present day.
Heaton Hall, Heaton Park   Tel 061 773 1231   Eighteenth-century furniture, silver, Etruscan room, wall-paintings. Pictures and sculpture.
Manchester Museum, The University, Oxford Road   Tel 061 273 3333 Archaeology, botany, geology, entomology, ethnology, numismatics. Aquarium and Vivarium. **Apply to the Teacher-in-charge.*
Queen's Park Art Gallery, Rochdale Road, Harpurley
Tel 061 205 2121   Dolls and dolls' houses. Regimental museum. Paintings and sculpture.
Whitworth Art Gallery, Whitworth Park   Tel 061 273 1880
See chapter 3.
Wythenshawe Hall, Wythenshawe Park, Northenden
Tel 061 998 2331   Furniture, pottery, paintings. Local interest items.

Oldham
Art Gallery and Museum, Union Street   Tel 061 624 3633   Glass,
Oriental collection, pictures and sculpture.
*Werneth Park Study Centre, Werneth Park, Frederick Street
Tel 061 624 2938*   Aquarium. Natural history collection.

Preston
Harris Museum and Art Gallery, Market Square   Tel Preston 53989
Ceramics, costume, dolls, glass, Victoriana. Local archaeology and
history. Pictures and sculpture.

Radcliffe
Local History Museum, Stand Lane   Tel 061 723 2344   Local
history, past and present. Changing art exhibitions.

Rawtenstall
Museum and Art Gallery, Whitaker Park   Tel Rossendale 4556
Natural history. Relics. Fine arts. Summer exhibitions.

Ribchester
Museum of Roman Antiquities. National Trust   Tel Ribchester 261
Pottery, coins, lamps, brooches. Model of Roman fort. Roman well and
granary in garden.

Rufford
Old Hall and Folk Museum. National Trust   Furniture, arms, armour,
costume, tools, china, dolls, children's games, local crafts.

St Helen's
Pilkington Glass Museum, Prescot Road   Tel St Helen's 28882   Glass
making through the ages. Ancient Egyptian god-figure. English and
Continental craftsmanship.
Public Art Gallery and Museum, Central Library   Tel St Helen's 24061
British birds, corals, glass, and local history. Annual art and camera club
exhibitions.

Salford
Science Museum, Buile Hill Park   Natural history, mining technology.

Southport
Botanic Gardens Museum, Churchtown   Tel Southport 87547   British
birds. Liverpool porcelain. Victorian period room. Local history.

Turton
Ashworth Museum, Turton Tower, Chapletown Road   Tel Turton 203
Local records, brass, furniture, weapons.

Warrington
Museum and Art Gallery, Bold Street   Tel Warrington 30550
Anthropology, botany, geology, ethnology, natural history. Glass, pottery, weapons, pictures.

Wigan
Art Gallery and Museum, Station Road   Tel Wigan 41387-9
Geology, mineralogy, coins, medals, local items and industries. Pictures. Frequent loan exhibitions.

LEICESTERSHIRE

Leicester
Belgrave Hall, Thurcaston Road   Tel Leicester 61610   Eighteenth-century furniture. Agricultural collection. Coaches.
Jewry Wall Museum, St Nicholas Street   Tel Leicester 22392
Archaeology. Mosaic pavement. Roman baths.
Museum and Art Gallery, New Walk   Tel Leicester 26832-3-4
Aquarium. Biology and geology. Ceramics, pictures and sculpture.
Newarke Houses Museum, The Newarke   Tel Leicester 580 988-9
Social history of city and county from 1500 to present day. Street scene, costumes, clocks, hosiery industry. Regimental Museum.
Railway Museum, London Road, Stoneygate   Local railway history items. Four locomotives. *Apply to Keeper of Schools Service, Belgrave House, Church Road, Belgrave, Leicester.*   Saturday club.

Market Harborough
*Archaeological and Historical Society Museum, The County Library
Tel Market Harborough 2649*   Local archaeology and history collections.

LINCOLNSHIRE

Boston
Boston Museum, The Guildhall, South Street   Local archaeology and history. Pictures.

Gainsborough
Old Hall, Parnell Street   Tel Gainsborough 2669 (afternoons) 3349 (evenings)   Folk museum. Furniture, china, coins, dolls, costume.

Grimsby
Central Library, Town Hall Square   Tel Grimsby 59161   Local and
travelling exhibitions.
Doughty Museum, Town Hall Square   Tel Grimsby 59161   Over sixty
model ships. China. Local interest items. Paintings.

Lincoln
City and County Museum, Broadgate   Tel Lincoln 30401/28621
Local archaeology, natural history, arms and armour.
Museum of Lincolnshire Life, County Centre, Burton Road
Tel Lincoln 26866   Historic material from Elizabeth I to present day.
Usher Gallery, Lindum Road   Tel Lincoln 27980/28621   Porcelain,
miniatures, watches. Lord Tennyson relics. Pictures.

Scunthorpe
Borough Museum and Art Gallery, Oswald Road   Tel Scunthorpe 3533
Archaeology, geology, natural history and industry. Period rooms. Art
exhibitions.

Spalding
Ayscoughfee Hall, Churchgate   Tel Spalding 2750   Natural history
museum, including British birds.
Spalding Museum, Broad Street   Tel Spalding 4658   Ceramics, glass,
coins, prehistoric relics.

LONDON

*Bethnal Green Museum (Victoria and Albert Museum), Cambridge
Heath Road, E2   Tel 01 980 2415*   Glass, pottery, silks. Toys and
dolls (made from wax, stone, straw, wood and bread). Holiday activities
and Saturday children's club. Δ *Apply to Education Officer.*
British Museum, Great Russell Street, WC1   Tel 01 636 1555
See chapter 3.
*British Museum (Department of Ethnography) Museum of Mankind,
6 Burlington Gardens, W1   Tel 01 437 2224-8*   For details of
exhibits see chapter 3.
Broomfield Museum, Broomfield Park, Palmers Green, N13
Tel 01 882 1354   Antiquities, natural history, pottery and paintings.
Butler Museum, Harrow School, Harrow-on-the-Hill, Middlesex
Tel 01 422 1465   Natural history, herbs and tropical lepidoptera.
The Church Farm House Museum, Church End, Hendon, NW4
Tel 01 203 0130   Period rooms. Local history. Special exhibitions.
Commonwealth Institute, Kensington High Street, W8
Tel 01 602 3252   See chapter 3.

Cuming Museum, Walworth Road, Southwark, SE17
Tel 01 703 3324/5529 Local archaeology, history, London
superstitions.

Epping Forest Museum, Queen Elizabeth's Hunting Lodge, Chingford,
E4 Animals, birds and plant life.

Fenton House, The Grove, Hampstead, NW3 *Tel 01 435 3471*
Porcelain, furniture and musical instruments.

Forty Hall Museum, Forty Hill, Enfield, Middlesex *Tel 01 363 8196*
Local history, furniture, pictures, exhibitions.

Geffrye Museum, Kingsland Road, Shoreditch, E2 *Tel 01 739 8368*
Period rooms from 1600. Temporary exhibitions. Holiday activities.
Δ *Apply to Schools Organiser.* Children's centre. Films.

Geological Museum, Exhibition Road, South Kensington, SW7
Tel 01 589 3444 See chapter 3.

Greenwich Borough Museum, 232 Plumstead High Street, SE18
Tel 01 854 1728 History, natural history and industry.

Guildhall Museum, Gillet House, 55 Basinghall Street, EC2
Tel 01 606 3030 Archaeology and history. Leathercraft, glass and
pottery.

Gunnersbury Park Museum, Gunnersbury Park, W3 *Tel 01 992 2247*
Archaeology, local history and relics. Coaches.

Ham House (Victoria and Albert Museum), Petersham, Richmond
Tel 01 940 1950 Stuart furniture, costumes and textiles. Pictures.

Hampton Court Palace, Hampton Court *Tel 01 977 8441* State
rooms, tapestries and pictures.

Hayes and Harlington Museum, Golden Crescent, Hayes, Middlesex
Tel 01 573 2855 Local history.

Horniman Museum, London Road, Forest Hill, SE23
Tel 01 699 2339/1872 Anthropology, ethnography, natural history
and musical instruments. Pottery facilities, etc in purpose-built centre
with children's tea room. Saturday morning Club and Christmas holiday
lectures. Δ*Apply to Schools Officer.*

Imperial War Museum, Lambeth Road, SE1 *Tel 01 735 8922*
See chapter 3.

Kingston-upon-Thames Museum and Art Gallery, Fairfield West
Tel 01 546 8905 Local archaeology, history and natural history.

London Museum, Kensington Palace, The Broadwalk, Kensington
Gardens, W8 *Tel 01 937 9816* See chapter 3.

Museum of London, London Wall (Purpose built museum) (to open
in November 1975) A chronological story of London with newly
acquired exhibits and ones from the Guildhall and the London Museum.
The Lord Mayor's coach and harness; royal robes; models. Classrooms,
including art and craft facilities and study areas, Library Refectory,
Weekend and holiday activities. Teacher training courses on how to use

museums. Facilities for invalids. ⌂ *Apply to the Education Officer, Education wing.*
London Transport Collection   Syon Park, Brentford.
Madame Tussaud's, Baker Street, NW1   See chapter 3.
Martinware Pottery Collection, Public Library, Osterley Park Road, Southall, Middlesex   Tel 01 574 3412   Birds, face mugs and other pottery pieces.
National Army Museum, Royal Hospital Road, Chelsea, SW3
Tel 01 730 0717   Ceramics, silver, relics, uniforms and decorations. Skeleton of Napoleon's horse. History of British Army 1485–1914. Later dates dealt with at the Imperial War Museum. This is one of the latest purpose-built museums, with imaginative and colourful display.
National Gallery, Trafalgar Square, WC2   Tel 01 839 3321
See chapter 3.
Natural History Museum, Cromwell Road, SW7   See chapter 3.
National Maritime Museum, Romney Road, Greenwich SE10
Tel 01 858 4583   See chapter 3.
National Portrait Gallery, St Martin's Place, Trafalgar Square, WC2
Tel 01 930 8511   See chapter 3.
Osterley House (Victoria and Albert Museum), Isleworth
Tel 01 560 3918   Decorations and furniture. Robert Adam work.
Passmore Edwards Museum, Romford Road, Stratford, E15
Tel 01 534 4545   Essex archaeology, geology and natural history. Holiday activities. *Apply to Assistant Curator (Extension Services).*
Percival David Foundation of Chinese Art, 53 Gordon Square, WC1
Tel 01 387 3909   Ceramics, art and culture.
St John's Gate, St John's Square, Clerkenwell, EC1   Tel 01 253 6644
Furniture, silver, treasures and pictures.
Science Museum (British Museum), Exhibition Road, South Kensington, SW7   Tel 01 589 6371   See chapter 3.
Sir John Soane's Museum, 13 Lincoln's Inn Fields, WC2
Tel 01 405 2107   Antiquities and works of art.
Tate Gallery, Millbank, SW1   Tel 01 828 1212   See chapter 3.
Tower of London, Tower Hill, EC3   Tel 01 709 0765   See chapter 3.
Victoria and Albert Museum, Cromwell Road, South Kensington, SW7
Tel 01 589 6371   See chapter 3.
Wallace Collection, Hertford House, Manchester Square, W1
Tel 01 935 0687   See chapter 3.
Walthamstow Museum, Vestry House, E17   Tel 01 527 5544   Local history and relics.
Wellington Museum (Victoria and Albert Museum), Apsley House, Hyde Park Corner, W1   Tel 01 499 5676   Trophies, uniforms, decorations and paintings. Relics of the ' Iron Duke '. Large marble statue of Napoleon. Famous Portuguese service of silver plate (presented

by the Regent of Portugal), took 142 craftsmen three years to make.

NORFOLK

Aylsham
Blickling Hall Furniture, pictures, tapestries.

Glandford
Glandford Museum and Trust Fund Shells from all over the world. Jewels, pottery and relics from Pompeii.

Great Yarmouth
Maritime Museum for East Anglia, Marine Parade Maritime history displays.
Museum of Domestic Life, 4 South Quay Tudor House, furniture, exhibitions of local interest.
Old Merchant's House, Row 117 Domestic ironwork collection, seventeenth to nineteenth centuries.
The Tolhouse, Tolhouse Street Local history. Dungeons.

King's Lynn
Museum and Art Gallery, Market Street *Tel King's Lynn 3596*
Regional archaeology, geology and natural history. Folk material, costumes, coins, glass and pottery. Pictures.

Norwich
Bridewell Museum of Local Industries and Rural Crafts, Bridewell Alley
Tel Norwich 22233 Industrial and rural crafts exhibits. Tools. Early bicycles and tricycles.
Castle Museum *Tel Norwich 22233* Local archaeology and natural history. Dioramas. Pictures. Loan exhibitions. Δ *Apply to Museums Education Officer.*
St Peter Hungate Church Museum, Princes Street *Tel Norwich 22233*
Church art, musical instruments and East Anglian antiquities.
Strangers Hall, Charing Cross *Tel Norwich 22233* Furniture, domestic life in sixteenth to nineteenth centuries.

Thetford
Ancient House Museum, White Hart Street *Tel Thetford 2297–8*
Archaeology, botany, entomology and zoology. Saxon pottery.

NORTHAMPTONSHIRE

Kettering
Westfield Museum, West Street *Tel Kettering 2315* Regional

archaeology and natural history. Shoe industry and tools.

Northampton
Abington Museum, Abington Park   Tel Northampton 31454   Period rooms. Ceramics. Victorian ' street '. Ethnography and natural history. *Central Museum and Art Gallery, Guildhall Road   Tel Northampton 34881 (daytime) 39131 (evenings and weekends)*   Local archaeology, ceramics, footwear. Historical collection. Pictures.

Peterborough
Museum and Art Gallery, Priestgate   Tel Peterborough 3329   Local archaeology, geology and natural history. Carved bonework and straw marquetry. Ceramics. Pictures.

Sulgrave
Sulgrave Manor   Ancestral home of George Washington. Relics. Period kitchen and kitchen equipment.

NORTHUMBERLAND

Berwick-on-Tweed
Museum and Art Gallery, Marygate   Tel Berwick-on-Tweed 7320   Silver, bronze, brass, glass and ceramics. Local antiquities. Paintings.

Chesters
The Clayton Collection, Hadrian's Wall, near Chollerford   Tel Chesters 379   Ornaments, weapons, tools from regional forts.

Corbridge
Corbridge Roman Site   Tel Corbridge 2349   Various Roman objects, pottery and sculpture.

Housesteads
Housesteads Museum, Haydon Bridge   Tel Bardon Mill 363   Roman objects, pottery and sculpture.

Lindisfarne
Lindisfarne Priory, Holy Island   Tel Holy Island 200   Medieval pottery, Anglo-Saxon sculpture. Reproduction of Lindisfarne gospels.

Newcastle upon Tyne
Greek Museum, The University, Percy Building, The Quadrangle   Tel Newcastle upon Tyne 28511   Greek and Etruscan art. Armour, bronzes, gems, terracottas.

Hancock Museum, The University, Barras Bridge Tel Newcastle upon Tyne 22359 Ethnography, natural history and original drawings by Thomas Bewick.
John G. Joicey Museum, City Road Tel Newcastle upon Tyne 24562 Armour, furniture, local history.
Laing Art Gallery and Museum, Higham Place Tel Newcastle upon Tyne 27734/26989 Egyptian and Greek antiquities. Pottery, glass, silver, ironwork, costumes, textiles. Local history. Pictures.
Mining Engineering Museum, The University, Queen Victoria Road Tel Newcastle upon Tyne 28511 History of mining, safety lamps and mine paintings.
Museum of Antiquities, The University, The Quadrangle Tel Newcastle upon Tyne 21727 Regional antiquities. Scale models.

NOTTINGHAMSHIRE

Mansfield
Museum and Art Gallery, Leeming Street Tel Mansfield 22561 Zoology. Lustre ware. Loan exhibitions of art, embroidery and sculpture.

Newark-on-Trent
Museum and Art Gallery, Appleton Gate Tel Newark-on-Trent 2358 Local archaeology, natural history and history. Coin hoards. Temporary exhibitions.

Nottingham
City Museum and Art Gallery, The Castle Tel Nottingham 43615 Ceramics, costumes, glass, lace, embroidery, textiles, wood and ironwork. Nottingham artists' pictures. **Apply to Museum Service Organiser, County Educational Museum Service, Gedling House, Wood Lane, Gedling, Nottingham.*
Natural History Museum, Wollaton Hall, Nottingham Tel 0602 281 333 Zoology, botany, geology. *Apply Schools Museum

Worksop
Worksop Museum, Memorial Avenue Tel Worksop 2408 Local archaeology, history and natural history. Victoriana. Sculpture.

OXFORDSHIRE

Banbury
Public Museum and Globe Room, Marlborough Road Tel Banbury 2282 Local history collection.

Holiday competition entry drawn with felt tip pens by John Carter aged 13. This was based on the temporary exhibition *Richard III* at the National Portrait Gallery illustrating a manuscript chronicle showing events in the King's life. The sheet of paper issued for the competition had the Gallery's portrait of the monarch reproduced on it

The Queen's House, Greenwich. Great Hall
National Maritime Museum

Burford
Tolsey Museum, High Street History of England. Eighteenth-century rooms with period furnishings and costumes in dolls' house. Local industries.

Oxford
Ashmolean Museum of Art and Archaeology, Beaumont Street Tel Oxford 57522 Archaeological exhibits. Ceramics, bronzes, silver, miniatures, tapestries, lacquer, coins, medals, marbles and metalwork. Pictures.
Museum of the History of Science, Broad Street Tel Oxford 43997 Early astronomical, mathematical and optical instruments. Geological, botanical, ethnological and zoological exhibits (Elias Ashmole's collection).
Oxford University Museum, Parks Road Tel Oxford 57467 Entomology, geology, mineralogy and zoology.
Pitt Rivers Museum, Parks Road Tel Oxford 54979 Prehistoric archaeology and ethnology. Musical instruments.

Woodstock
Oxford City and County Museum, Fletcher's House Tel Woodstock 811456 Crafts, industries. Oxford city and county life. Temporary exhibitions. *Apply to Museum Education Officer.*

RUTLAND

Oakham
Rutland County Museum, Catmos Street Tel Oakham 3654 Archaeology, craft tools, agricultural implements, local history.

SHROPSHIRE

Aston Munslow
The White House Country Life Museum, near Craven Arms Agricultural tools, implements, domestic and dairy utensils. Cart house, stable, cider mill and press.

Coalbrook Dale
Museum of Ironfounding History of iron casting and smelting. Furnace, locomotives and steam engines, machinery, street furniture.

Ludlow
Ludlow Museum, Butter Cross Tel Ludlow 2619 20,000 Shropshire fossils. Local history, arms, armour.

I

Shrewsbury
Clive House, College Hill   Tel Shrewsbury 54811   Art, ceramics, furniture, geological exhibits. Regimental Museum.
Rowley's House Museum, Barker Street   Tel Shrewsbury 54876
Prehistoric, medieval and geological exhibits.

Wroxeter
Viroconium Museum   Tel Wroxeter 330   Roman coins, objects, pottery.

SOMERSET

Bath
American Museum in Britain, Claverton Manor, near Bath   Tel Bath 60503   Glass, textiles, hat-boxes, folk sculpture, patchwork quilts. Furnished rooms. Marine section. *Apply to Director of Education* (for older students) or *The Secretary, John Judkyn Memorial, Freshford Manor, Bath.*
Holburne of Menstrie Museum, Great Pulteney Street   Tel Bath 3669
Glass, furniture, porcelain, silver, miniatures, paintings.
Museum of Costume, Assembly Rooms   Tel Bath 28411   Fashion from the seventeenth century to the present day.
Victoria Art Gallery, Bridge Street   Tel Bath 28144   Ceramics, glass, coins, watches and pictures. Special exhibitions.

Bridgwater
Admiral Blake Museum, Blake Street   Tel Bridgwater 2597   Relics. Battle of Sedgemoor exhibits. Archaeology, local history, shipping.

Cheddar
Veteran and Vintage Car Museum, The Cliffs   Tel Cheddar 742446
Cars, motor cycles, steam engines, accessories. Discovery of caves section.

Glastonbury
Glastonbury Lake Village Museum, The Tribunal, High Street   Local archaeology and history.

Shepton Mallet
Shepton Mallet Museum, Market Place   Relics of early man. Medieval, geological, ornithological and palaeontological collections.

Taunton
Somerset County Museum, Taunton Castle   Tel Taunton 3451   Local and natural history, geology, archaeology, pewter, pottery, glass, dolls,

working engines. Aquaria. *Apply to the Tutor Organiser, Somerset Educational Museum and Art Service, Weir Lodge, Staplegrove Road, Taunton.*

Wells
Wells Museum, Cathedral Green   Tel Wells 3477   Natural history, minerals, coins, local and prehistoric objects.

Weston-super-Mare
Museum and Art Gallery, The Boulevard   Tel Weston-Super-Mare 24133   Local archaeology, agricultural and domestic objects. Somerset birds. Special exhibitions.

Wookey Hole
Wookey Hole Caves Museum   Animal and human bones, cooking utensils, jewellery. Glass, pottery, ornaments and tools. Miniature works of art.

Yeovil
Borough Museum, Hendford Manor Hall   Tel Yeovil 3144
Archaeology, industry, costume and firearms.

STAFFORDSHIRE

Bilston
Bilston Museum and Art Gallery, Mount Pleasant   Local and regional history. Pictures. Various loan collections exhibited.

Blithfield
Museum of Childhood and Costume, Blithfield Hall, near Rugeley Tel Dappleheath 249   Victorian dolls' houses, toy and miniature theatres. Children's books, toys, furniture and costumes. Needlework figures.

Burton-on-Trent
Museum and Art Gallery, Guild Street   Tel Burton-on-Trent 3042
Local history. British and foreign birds. Travelling art exhibitions.

Lichfield
Art Gallery and Museum, Bird Street   Tel Lichfield 2177   Local history. Picture loan service. Temporary art exhibitions.

Newcastle-under-Lyme
Borough Museum and Art Gallery, Brampton Park   Tel Newcastle-

under-Lyme 619705 Local history, geology, natural history and science. Ceramics, textiles, Arab and Shorter Oriental collections. Pictures.

Shugborough
County Museum and Mansion House, Great Haywood, near Stafford Tel Littlehaywood 388 Vehicles, railway and industrial exhibits. Silver, costume, pottery, furniture. Geology. Pictures.

Stafford
Museum and Art Gallery, The Green Tel Stafford 2151 Local history, social life, industry. Picture loan service. Changing art exhibitions.

Stoke-on-Trent
Museum and Art Gallery, Broad Street, Hanley Tel Stoke-on-Trent 22714 International pottery collection. Archaeology, and natural history. Costumes, dolls, samplers. Pictures and sculpture.

Tamworth
Castle Museum, The Holloway Tel Tamworth 3561 Saxon and Norman coins. Local history. Glass. Pictures.

Walsall
E. M. Flint Art Gallery, Lichfield Street Local history. Leathercraft and locks. Exhibitions of pictures.

Wolverhampton
Art Gallery and Museum, Lichfield Street Tel Wolverhampton 24549 Enamels and pottery. Pictures and sculpture.
Bantock House, Bantock Park Tel Wolverhampton 24548 Porcelain, ivories, various objects.

SUFFOLK

Bury St Edmunds
The Gershom-Parkington Memorial Collection of Clocks and Watches, 8 Angel Hill Clocks and instruments from sixteenth century onwards.
Moyse's Hall Museum, Cornhill Tel Bury St Edmunds 2375 Local antiquities, natural history, thirteenth-century Monk's Chronicle.

Ipswich
Christchurch Mansion, Christchurch Park Tel Ipswich 53246 Period rooms. Porcelain, glass. Pictures by Suffolk artists. Modern original prints.

Ipswich Museum, High Street   Tel Ipswich 213761–2   Regional archaeology, geology, ethnography and natural history. **Apply to Educational Liaison Officer.*

Southwold
Southwold Museum, St Bartholomew's Green   Tel Southwold 3536 Local archaeology, natural history and relics.

Stowmarket
The Abbot's Hall Museum of Rural Life of East Anglia Tel Stowmarket 2229   Agriculture, crafts, domestic utensils.

SURREY

Camberly
Camberley Museum, Knoll Road   Tel Camberley 64483   Local archaeology, history and natural history.

Farnham
Farnham Museum, Willmer House, 38 West Street   Tel Farnham 5094 Local archaeology, furniture, clocks, costumes, glass paperweights. Relics associated with local famous men.

Godalming
Charterhouse School Museum   Tel Godalming 681   Archaeology, geology and natural history. Costume, glass, furniture, pottery and silver.

Guildford
Museum and Muniment Room, Castle Arch   Tel Guildford 66551 Regional archaeology and history. Ironwork and needlework.

Haslemere
Haslemere Educational Museum, High Street   Tel Haslemere 65902 Geology, natural history, local history and industries. Weekend field courses, Saturday morning club. **Apply to the Curator.*

Reigate
Holmesdale Natural History Club Museum, 14 Croydon Road Tel Reigate 66552   British birds, fossils, insects, minerals.

Weybridge
Weybridge Museum, Church Street   Tel Weybridge 43573   Local archaeology, history and costume.

SUSSEX

Battle
Battle Museum, Langton House   Diorama. Roman-British remains.
Sussex iron industry collection.

Bexhill
Bexhill Museum, Egerton Park   Tel Bexhill 1769   Local archaeology,
geology and natural history. Frequent loan exhibitions.

Bignor
Bignor Roman Villa Collection   Coins, jewellery, pottery and models.

Bodiam
Castle Museum   Relics from excavations.

Bognor Regis
Guermonprez Museum, Lyon Street   Tel Bognor Regis 3141
Archaeology, local history and natural science.

Brighton
Booth Museum of British Birds, Dyke Road   Tel Brighton 552586
Birds, eggs, butterflies and moths.
Tel Brighton 63005   Archaeology, natural history, folk life. Ceramics,
Museum and Art Gallery, Northgate House, Church Street
glass, jewellery, musical instruments. Pictures. Frequent temporary
exhibitions. **Apply to Schools Service Officer.* School loan service.
Preston Manor, Preston Park   Tel Brighton 552101   Furniture, china,
silver and leather hangings.
The Royal Pavilion   Tel Brighton 63005   23 furnished state rooms,
including King George IV's Apartments, Banqueting Room, and Great
Kitchen.

Chichester
City Museum, 29 Little London   Tel Chichester 84683   Local
archaeology and history. Furniture. Diorama. Royal Sussex Regiment
collection.

Eastbourne
Royal National Lifeboat Institution Museum, Grand Parade
Tel Eastbourne 4717   Lifeboats past and present, including objects
connected with them.

Tower, 73 The Wish Tower, King Edward's Parade   Tel Eastbourne 35809   Napoleonic war weapons, uniforms and equipment.
Towner Art Gallery, 9 Borough Lane   Tel Eastbourne 21635   British butterflies, caricatures, original prints, paintings, sculpture. Frequent temporary exhibitions.

Hastings
Museum and Art Gallery, John's Place, Cambridge Road   Tel Hastings 1952   Ethnography, local history and relics. Ceramics, pottery and ironwork. Temporary art exhibitions.
Museum of Local History, Old Town Hall, High Street   Local history and relics. Model ships.

Horsham
Horsham Museum, Causeway House   Local history, crafts and industry. Reconstructed places of work. Early bicycles, toys and costumes.

Hove
Museum of Art, Central Library, Church Road   Ceramics, furniture, glass, silver. Toys, dolls and dolls' houses. Picture loan scheme, film strips and transparencies.

Lewes
Anne of Cleves House, High Street, Southover   Costumes, furniture, fossils, ironwork, relics.
Barbican House Museum, High Street   Tel Lewes 4379   Regional antiquities. Prints and watercolours. *Apply to Schools Museum Organiser, Baron's Down, Brighton Road, Lewes.*

Littlehampton
Littlehampton Museum, 12A River Road   Tel Littlehampton 5149   Local interest objects, sailing and marine exhibits.

Rottingdean
Grange Art Gallery and Museum   Sussex folk life collection. Toys. Frequent temporary displays in art gallery.

Rye
Rye Museum, Ypres Tower   Local history, pottery and Victoriana.

Shoreham
The Marlipins Museum, High Street   Local history, archaeology and geology. Model ships and paintings.

Singleton
The Open Air Museum, near Chichester   Historic buildings. ' Bayleaf ', fifteenth-century farmhouse on 38-acre site. Traditional crafts and rural industries. Woodland nature trail.

West Hoathly
Priest House   Dolls, embroideries, furniture and relics.

Winchelsea
Winchelsea Museum, Court Hall   Local history, archaeology, crafts, models.

Worthing
Museum and Art Gallery, Chapel Road   *Tel Worthing 39189*   Local archaeology and geology. Dolls, jewellery, praxinoscope theatre, costume, pottery and model ships. Pictures.

WARWICKSHIRE

Birmingham
Blakesley Hall, Blakesley Road, Yardley   *Tel 021 783 2193*   Period rooms. Local archaeology and history.
Cannon Hill Museum, Pershore Road   *Tel 021 472 0811*   Natural history. Dioramas. Safari hut.
City Museum and Art Gallery, Congreve Street   *Tel 021 535 2834*   See chapter 3.
Geological Departmental Museum, The University, Edgbaston   *Tel 021 472 1301*   Minerals. Fossils.
Museum of Science and Industry, Newhall Street   *Tel 021 236 1022*   Engineering exhibits. Transport. Music collection. Small arms. Temporary exhibitions.

Coventry
Herbert Art Gallery and Museum, Jordan Well   *Tel Coventry 25555*   Local natural history and industry. Frequent loan exhibitions in art gallery.

Leamington Spa
Art Gallery and Museum, Avenue Road   *Tel Leamington Spa 25873*   Pottery and glass. Pictures.

Nuneaton
Museum and Art Gallery, Riversley Park   *Tel Nuneaton 2683*   Local archaeology, geology and ethnography. Glass, pottery and silver.

Stratford-upon-Avon
Mary Arden's House, Wilmcote Tel Stratford-upon-Avon 4016
Sixteenth-century furniture. Agricultural implements and relics.
New Place and Nash's House Tel Stratford-upon-Avon 4016 Local
history, antiquities and David Garrick exhibits.
Royal Shakespeare Theatre Picture Gallery Set designs, costumes, wigs,
masks and head-dresses. Portraits.

Warwick
County Museum, Market Place Tel Warwick 43431 Local
archaeology, geology, history and natural history. Changing loan
exhibitions. *Apply to Schools Services Assistant.*
Doll Museum, Oken's House, Castle Street Dolls and toys.
St John's House, Coten End Tel Warwick 43431 Costumes, furniture,
loan exhibitions.

WESTMORLAND

Kendal
Abbot Hall Art Gallery Tel Kendal 22464–5 Furniture, pottery,
sculpture, paintings. Changing exhibitions.
Abbot Hall Museum Costume, period rooms, industry. Opportunities
for children's creative work in conjunction with museum activities.
Borough Museum, Station Road Tel Kendal 21374 Local and natural
history.

WILTSHIRE

Avebury
*Alexander Keiller Museum, Ministry of Public Works and Buildings
Tel Avebury 250* Objects and pottery from local excavations.

Devizes
Devizes Museum, Long Street Tel Devizes 2765 Regional
archaeology and geology. Bronze Age ornaments and utensils.

Malmesbury
Athelstan Museum, Cross Hayes Tel Malmesbury 2143 Local objects,
household articles and old fire-engine.

Salisbury
Salisbury and South Wiltshire Museum, St Ann Street Regional,
natural and social history. Models. Costumes, crafts, glass and pottery.

Swindon
Museum and Art Gallery, Bath Road   Tel Swindon 27211   Regional archaeology, botany, geology, and natural history. Musical instruments. Travelling exhibitions.

WORCESTERSHIRE

Dudley
Museum and Art Gallery, St James's Road   Tel Dudley 56321
Geology. Regional life and history. Temporary exhibitions. Pictures.

Evesham
Almonry Museum, Vine Street   Agricultural implements. Local history. Roman-British, Anglo-Saxon, medieval and monastic remains.

Kidderminster
Kidderminster Museum, Market Street   Local archaeology.
Worcestershire County Museum, Hartlebury Castle, near Kidderminster Tel Kidderminster 63610   Archaeology, geology, craft and industries. Costume, glass and furniture. Horse-drawn vehicles. Georgian furnished room. Eighteenth-century kitchen equipment. *Apply to Museum Education Officer.*

Worcester
City Museum and Art Gallery, Foregate Street   Tel Worcester 22154/ 24853   Regional archaeology, geology and natural history. Folk life. Worcestershire Regiment collection. Art gallery, travelling exhibitions.

YORKSHIRE

Aldborough
Aldborough Roman Museum, Boroughbridge   Tel Aldborough 2768
Roman finds. Glass, coins, metalwork and pottery.

Barnsley
Cannon Hall Art Gallery and Museum, Cawthorne   Tel Silkstone 270
Period rooms. China, furniture, silver and paintings. Military section.

Batley
Bagshaw Museum, Wilton Park   Tel Batley 2514   Local archaeology, history, natural history. Antiquities, textiles, Victoriana. Temporary exhibitions.

Beverley
Art Gallery and Museum, Champrey Road   Tel Beverley 882255
Local antiquities. Pictures.

Bradford
City Art Gallery and Museum, Cartwright Hall   Tel Bradford 48247–8
Regional archaeology, geology and natural history. Electric tramcars and
industrial machine models. Pictures. **Apply to The Keeper, Museums'
Education Service.*

Bridlington
Art Gallery and Museum, Sewerby Hall   Tel Bridlington 2917   Amy
Johnson exhibition. Archaeology and natural history. Loan exhibitions of
art.
Bayle Museum, Augustinian Priory   Relics, weapons, jewellery, dolls,
model boats. Pictures. *Correspondence to Reighton Hall, Filey, East
Yorks.*

Castleford
Public Library and Museum, Carlton Street   Tel Castleford 3553
Roman exhibits, Castleford glass and pottery.

Cawthorne
Victoria Jubilee Museum, near Barnsley   Geology, natural history and
local objects.

Dewsbury
Museum and Art Gallery, Crow Nest Park   Tel Dewsbury 1261
Natural history and local history. Travelling art exhibitions.

Doncaster
Museum and Art Gallery, Chequer Road   Tel Doncaster 60814   Local
history, natural history. Roman-British exhibits, costume. Frequent
temporary art exhibitions.

Halifax
Bankfield Museum and Art Gallery, Akroyd Park   Tel Halifax 54823
Archaeology, local history and natural history. Costume and textiles.
Regimental museum.
*West Yorkshire Folk Museum, Shibden Hall, Shibden Park   Tel Halifax
52246*   Furniture, agricultural implements, craft workshops, coaches.

Harrogate
*Royal Pump Room Museum, opposite Valley Gardens   Tel Harrogate
3340*   Archaeology, local history, costume, pottery and Victoriana.

Huddersfield

Tolson Memorial Museum, Ravensknowle Park, Wakefield Road
Tel Huddersfield 30591 Geology, botany, history and natural history.
Toys, vehicles, local industries.

Hull

Maritime Museum, Pickering Park Tel Hull 27625 Whaling relics.
Fishing and shipping.
Transport and Archaeology Museum, 36 High Street Tel Hull 27625
Regional archaeology. Coaches and motor cars.
*Apply to Keeper of School Services, Hull Museums, 23/24 High
Street, Hull. Saturday morning club.

Hutton-le-hole

Ryedale Folk Museum, Elphield Tel Lastingham 367 Antiquities.
Furniture, glass, tools, crafts.

Ilkley

Manor House Museum and Art Gallery, Castle Yard Tel Ilkley 2431
Local history, prehistoric times to present day. Pottery, paintings and
sculpture.

Keighley

Art Gallery and Museum, Cliffe Castle Tel Keighley 7139
Archaeology, geology, natural history. Craft workshops. Toys and
games. Applied arts, pictures and sculpture.

Leeds

Abbey House Museum, Kirkstall Tel Leeds 55821 Folk museum.
Full-sized nineteenth-century houses, shops. Costume, dolls, musical
instruments. **Apply to the Schools Museum Officer.*
City Museum, Municipal Buildings Tel Leeds 32628 Archaeology,
geology and natural history. Model coal pit. **Apply to the Schools*
Museum Officer.
Temple Newsom House Tel Leeds 647321 Ceramics, furniture, silver
and paintings.

Malton

Roman Malton Museum, Milton Rooms, Market Place Local Roman-
British collections, also prehistoric and medieval.

Pontefract

Castle Museum, Pontefract Castle Local relics, pottery, coins, weapons
and armour.

Rotherham
Museum and Art Gallery, Clifton Park   Tel Rotherham 5481
Antiquities and natural history. Gemstones, porcelain and pottery.
Nature trail. Annual Schools art exhibition. *Apply to Schools Officer,
Education Offices, Wellgate, Rotherham.*

Scarborough
Museum of Natural History, Wood End   Tel Scarborough 64285–6
Geology and natural history. Aquarium.
Scarborough Museum, Vernon Road   Tel Scarborough 64285–6
Regional archaeology and pottery.

Sheffield
City Museum, Weston Park   Tel Sheffield 27226   Geology,
archaeology and natural history. Ceramics, cutlery and old Sheffield
plate. *Apply to The Keeper, Extension Services.*
*Schools' Service Assistant, City Art Galleries, Weetwood, Knowle Lane,
Ecclesall Road South, Sheffield.*

Skipton
Craven Museum Library and Museum, High Street   Tel Skipton 2926
Geology, natural history, crafts and antiquities.

Wakefield
City Museum, Wood Street   Tel Wakefield 76403   Local and natural
history. Ceramics, costume, glass and silver. Period rooms and shops.
Apply to The Organiser, Museum Service, 71C Northgate, Wakefield.

Whitby
*Literary and Philosophical Society Museum, Pannett Park   Tel Whitby
2908*   Local and natural history and famous men. Roman relics.
Shipping gallery.

York
Castle Museum, Tower Street   Tel York 53611   Folk museum. Period
rooms. Crafts, costumes, toys and musical instruments.
City Art Gallery, Exhibition Square   Tel York 23839   Ceramics,
pottery, pictures and sculpture.
Yorkshire Museum, Museum Street   Tel York 29745   Archaeology,
geology, and natural history. Coins and pottery.

NORTHERN IRELAND

Armagh
County Museum, The Mall   Tel Armagh 2404   Local antiquities, weapons, costumes, uniforms. Natural history.

Belfast
Transport Museum, Witham Street, Newtownards Road   Tel Belfast 51519   Locomotives, trams, carriages, bicycles and fire appliances. Model ships. Pictures.
Ulster Folk Museum, Cultra Manor   Tel Holywood 3555 Local history.
Ulster Museum, Botanic Gardens,   Tel Belfast 668251 Natural history, Irish antiquities, paintings, archaeology, geology.

EIRE

Dublin
National Museum of Ireland, Leinster House, Kildare Street Tel Dublin 65521   Archaeology, antiquities, geology, botany and zoology. Folk life. Fine arts.
National Gallery, Merrion Square   European, Italian, and Irish paintings.

SCOTLAND

Aberdeen
Art Gallery and Museum, School Hill   Tel Aberdeen 23942   Textiles, stained glass, Chinese decorative art, pictures.
University Anthropological Museum   Tel Aberdeen 40241 Archaeology, ethnography and antiquities.
University Natural History Museum, Tillydrone Avenue   Tel Aberdeen 40241   Teaching and study collection.

Airdrie, Lanark
Airdrie Public Museum, Wellwynd   Tel Airdrie 3221   Local history. Regular exhibitions.

Annan, Dumfries
Annan Museum, Moat House   Archaeology, history, natural history.
Shipping.

Anstruther, Fife
Scottish Fisheries Museum, St Ayles, Harbourhead   Tel Anstruther 628
Marine aquarium, fishing gear, navigation, model ships.

Banff, Banffshire
Banff Museum   Tel Banff 2591   Antiquities, local and natural history.

Blair Atholl, Perth
Blair Castle and Atholl Museum   China, furniture, arms and armour,
torture instruments, portraits.

Campbeltown, Argyll
Campbeltown Museum, Public Library, Hall Street   Local archaeology,
geology and natural history.

Culross, Fife
Dunimarle Museum   Tel Newmills 229   Ceramics, glass, furniture and
silver.

Dumfries
Burgh Museum, The Observatory, Corberry Hill   Tel Dumfries 3374
Archaeology, history and natural history.

Dundee
City Museum and Art Galleries, Albert Square   Tel Dundee 25492–3
Regional archaeology, geology, botany, history and natural history.
Pictures.

Dunfermline, Fife
Dunfermline Museum, Viewfield   Tel Dunfermline 24404   Local
history and natural history. Art and travelling exhibitions.
Pittencrieff House Museum, Pittencrieff Park   Tel Dunfermline 22935
Past and present costumes. Temporary exhibitions connected with
costume.

Edinburgh
Huntly House, Canongate   Tel 031 556 0813   Local history. Glass
and pottery.
Lauriston Castle, Cramond Road South   Tel 031 336 3060
Ceramics, furniture, wool mosaics and tapestries.

Museum of Childhood, 38 High Street Tel 031 556 5447 Games, toys, costume, health and education.
National Museum of Antiquities of Scotland, Queen Street
Tel 031 556 8921 See chapter 3.
Royal Scottish Museum, Chambers Street Tel 031 225 7534
Archaeology, natural history, geology. Children's gallery. Pottery.*
Pictures. Technology Department with scale models which viewers can operate. *Apply to Schools Museum Officer, South Bridge Street, Infirmary Street, Edinburgh.*

Elgin
Elgin Museum, 1 High Street Tel Elgin 3675 Fossils, Stone and Bronze Age weapons, lepidoptera.

Falkirk, Stirlingshire
Burgh Museum, Dollar Park, Stirlingshire Archaeology and local history.

Forfar, Angus
Meffan Institute Museum, 20 West High Street Archaeology, geology, natural history. Burning of witches bridle.

Forres, Moray
Falconer Museum, Centre of Forres Tel Forres 25 Arrowheads, fossils, foreign collection.

Fort William, Inverness
West Highland Museum, Cameron Square History, natural history, relics and folk collection.

Glasgow
Art Gallery and Museum, Kelvingrove Tel 041 334 1134-5-6 See chapter 3.
Hunterian Museum, Glasgow University Tel 041 339 8855
Archaeology, geology, ethnography and history. Pictures.
Museum of Transport, 25 Albert Drive Tel 041 423 8000 Land transport, tramcars, vintage cars and horse-drawn vehicles.
Tollcross Museum, Tollcross Park Zoology. Dolls.

Glenesk, Angus
Folk Museum, The Retreat Tel Tarfside 236/256 Period rooms, costume, children's and farmer's rooms.

Greenock, Renfrew
The McLean Museum, 9 Union Street, West End   Tel Greenock 23741
Geology, natural history, model ships and engines.

Hawick, Roxborough
Inverurie Museum, Public Library Building, Aberdeen   Archaeology,
geology and natural history.
Wilton Lodge Museum, The Park   Tel Hawick 3457   Geology, natural
history, local history.

Kilmarnock, Ayrshire
Dick Institute Museum, Elmbank Avenue   Tel Kilmarnock 21144
Archaeology, geology, ethnology and ornithology. Children's museum.
Pictures.

Kircaldy, Fife
Museum and Art Gallery, War Memorial Grounds   Tel Kircaldy 2732
Local archaeology, geology and natural history. Pottery, pictures.

Millport, Isle of Cumbrae
*Robertson Museum and the Aquarium, Marine Station   Tel Millport
581-2*   Natural history and marine life.

Montrose, Angus
Montrose Museum, Panmure Place   Tel Montrose 615   Regional
archaeology, geology, history and natural history. Medals and coins.

North Berwick, East Lothian
Burgh Museum, The Old Public School   Archaeology, history and
natural history. Costumes and pottery.

Paisley, Renfrew
Museum and Art Galleries, High Street   Tel 041 889 3151   Regional
geology, history and natural history. Ceramics, shawls and manuscripts.
Pictures. *Apply Schools Service Officer.*

Peebles
Chambers Institution, High Street   Tel Peebles 20123   Botany, geology
and local history.

Perth
Art Gallery and Museum, George Street   Tel Perth 24241   Antiquities,
geology, ethnography and natural history. Tropical aquaria. Pictures.

K

Rothesay, Bute
Buteshire Natural History Society Museum, Stuart Street   Archaeology, geology, history and natural history.

St Andrews, Fife
Cathedral Museum   Glass, pottery and relics.

Saltcoats, Ayrshire
North Ayrshire Museum, Kirkgate   Regional history, industry and life.

Stirling
Smith Art Gallery and Museum, Albert Place   Tel Stirling 2849
Archaeology, ethnology and natural history. Pictures.

Stromness, Orkney
Orkney National History Museum, 52 Alfred Street   Tel Stromness 246
Botany, geology, ethnology, zoology. Model ships.

Thurso, Caithness
Thurso Museum, The Library   Tel Thurso 3237   Botany, geology and zoology.

Wick, Caithness
Carnegie Library and Museum   Tel Wick 2864   Local antiquities and natural history.

WALES

Abergavenny, Monmouth
Abergavenny and District Museum, Castle House   Archaeology. Dolls, costumes, farm tools.

Aberystwyth, Cardigan
University College of Wales, Museum and Art Gallery
Tel Aberystwyth 4235   Ceramics, glass and craftwork. Visiting exhibitions.

Bangor, Caernarvon
Museum of Welsh Antiquities, College Road   Tel Bangor 51151
Antiquities, ceramics, furniture and textiles.
Penrhyn Castle   Dolls, birds, butterflies and locomotives.

Brecon
Brecknock Museum, Glamorgan Street Archaeology and natural
history. Costume, coins, pottery and paintings.

Cardiff, Glamorgan
National Museum of Wales, Cathays Park Tel Cardiff 26241
See chapter 3.

Carmarthen
The County Museum, 5 Quay Street Tel Carmarthen 66141
Antiquities and neolithics.

Haverfordwest, Pembrokeshire
Pembrokeshire County Museum, The Castle Tel Haverfordwest 3708
Archaeology, industry and folk life. Frequent temporary exhibitions.

Llandrindod Wells, Radnorshire
*Radnorshire County Museum, Public Library, War Memorial Gardens,
Temple Street Tel Llandrindod Wells 2212* Archaeology, doll
collection and temporary exhibitions.

Llandudno, Caernarvon
*Rapallo House Museum and Art Gallery, Caernarvon Tel Llandudno
76517* Arms, relics, bronzes, sculpture, pictures.

Llanelli, Carmarthen
Parc Howard Museum and Art Gallery Tel Llanelli 2029 Pottery,
local items, pictures.

Llanidloes, Montgomery
*Museum of Local History and Industry, Market Hall Tel Llanidloes
368* Local interest objects and industry.

Merthyr Tydfil, Glamorgan
Art Gallery and Museum, Cyfarthfa Castle Tel Merthyr Tydfil 3112
Local history, natural history, ceramics, coins, china and silver. Welsh
kitchen. Pictures.

Monmouth
Nelson Museum, The Market Hall, Priory Street Tel Monmouth 2122
Local history and relics. China, glass, silver, ships and swords. Model of
Battle of Trafalgar.

Newport, Monmouth
Museum and Art Gallery, John Frost Square   Tel Newport 65781
Archaeology, natural history, japan ware. Pictures. *Apply to Schools
Services Officer.*

Penarth, Glamorgan
Turner House Gallery, Plymouth Road   Tel Penarth 708870   Applied
art and pictures.

Swansea
Glynn Vivian Art Gallery, Alexandra Road   Tel Swansea 55006
Ceramics, glass, paintings, sculpture. Loan exhibitions.
*Royal Institution of South Wales Museum, Victoria Road   Tel Swansea
53763*   Archaeology, geology, ornithology. Antiquities. Folk life. Art
and industry.

Tenby, Pembroke
Tenby Museum, Castle Hill   Tel Tenby 2809   Local archaeology,
geology, history and natural history.

It is interesting to compare the variations of design, texture, shape, and
colour in near similar items in other museums in the British Isles and
overseas. Some excel others in appearance, and it is intriguing to find out
why one object appears superior to another – a greater subtlety of design
or pure simplicity, a more even texture (either rough, matt, or shiny) in
pottery, a more satisfactory placing of arms related to head and legs in a
figure, or shapes in abstract works, pleasing contrasts (of dark and light
tones) more beautiful colours.

In pictures, textiles, or embroidery, the balance of shapes (abstract or
representational) to form an interesting composition, balance and choice
of colour, correct choice of design to fit the medium (be it oil, watercolour, wools, silks, fabrics), so that it is felt that no other would express
the combination as appropriately – in other words ' *truth* to medium '.
For instance, stone cannot be twisted into meticulous detailed shapes, but
bold main forms capable of translation within the whole by means of the
type of tools used.

From observing similar objects in museums, one can use the knowledge
gained to identify local architecture, and furniture and pictures in antique
shops. By looking for patterns which were typical of a certain period,
furniture, costume, wigs or hairstyles can all help to estimate the date of
a picture. Occasionally the artist's name can be found underneath the dark
paint on the left or right side bottom corners of the picture. This can then
be looked up in dictionaries of art – just in case the artist was a famous

one – there are still exciting discoveries in these days, in old attics and elsewhere.

Christies and Sotheby's and private auctioneers will give the approximate market value for a fee, if not for sale, and for nothing, if it is given them to sell with a percentage for the sale.

Museum terminology

Ages of man
>*Palaeolithic*   Old Stone Age. Use of primitive stone implements by nomads (hunting culture).
>*Neolithic*   Later or New Stone Age. Use of ground or polished stone weapons and implements by cave-dwellers (agricultural and herding cultures). Stonehenge was built during this period.
>*Bronze*   Use of metal celts. Arrival of the Beaker people, named after their drinking vessels. After the Bronze Age came the Iron Age.

Antiquities   Ancient relics.
Archaeology   Study of antiquities, especially of the prehistoric period.
Botany   Science of plants.
Biology   Science of physical life, animals and plants.
Ceramics   Earthenware, stoneware, or porcelain.
>*Earthenware*   Baked clay. Tin-glazed earthenware is known as *faience* in France, majolica in Italy and Spain, Delft in Holland.
>*Glaze*   A coat of glass (which consists of sand, flint or sandstone mixed with lead, borax or potash) which pottery is dipped in after initial firing. It is then fired again to form the hard glass-like surface. Metallic oxides are added to the glaze for different colours.
>*Porcelain*   China clay fused with china-stone: hard, thin and translucent pottery.
>*Slipware*   Earthenware decorated with ' slip ', a creamy clay wash: eg Thomas Toft's plates.
>*Spode bone-china*   A paste between hard and soft porcelain. White ash from burnt ox bones is used as one of the ingredients.
>*Stoneware*   This is fired at a very high temperature, often with the addition of salt to the kiln, producing a pleasant rough surface.
>*Terracotta*   Brownish-red clay.

Chinese dynasties   Periods of time when emperors ruled. Each of the following periods produced a distinctive style of art. Paintings, which idealised reality in flat stylised patterning, were usually on silk and paper – writing was often added.
>*T'ang Dynasty*   Horses, ducks, camels; figures, usually buried in the grave of some lord for the continuation of his afterlife. Made in metalwork and colour-glazed terracotta eathenware.
>*Chou Dynasty*   Bronze owls.

Han Dynasty Bronze, axle hub with dragon's head, mirrors, jade horse's heads.

Sung Dynasty Chinese porcelain, bowls and dishes.

Ming Dynasty Blue and white porcelain, flasks with dragons, serpentine marble horse.

Ching Dynasty Paintings by K'urs'an.

Shang Dynasty Bronze, ritual vessels, jade, textiles.

Classical Of ancient Rome or Greece.

Dioramas Small models of such places as villages and seaports, with figures.

Entomology Study of insects.

Ethnography Scientific description of races of men.

Ethnology Descriptive study of human cultures. Science of races, their characteristics and relation to one another.

Fossils Preserved remains of plants and animals, usually found in rocks.

Fresco Watercolour laid on wall or ceiling before plaster is dry.

Geology Science of the earth's crust, strata, their relations and changes.

Gouache Opaque colours ground in water and thickened with honey and gum.

Horology Art of measuring time or making clocks.

Lepidoptera Insects with four membranous scale-covered wings, including moths and butterflies.

Medieval Of the Middle Ages.

Mineralogy Science of minerals.

Numismatics The study of coins.

Papier mâché In the mid-eighteenth century a material composed of pulped paper, adding chalk and sand, was shaped by being pressed into boxwood moulds. Later, a composition was invented using flour, ground rags, glue and water. A process was patented in 1772 for making a tough, heat and moisture-resisting material which could be treated to acquire a surface lustre finish almost resembling lacquer. Coloured paints, including gold and bronze, were applied over the dried and varnished objects such as trays, tea-caddies, and boxes and then covered with shellac. These were hardened by heat and then rubbed with oil for a polished effect.

Palaeontology Study of organic life remains preserved in rocks.

Petrology Study of origin and structure of rocks.

Philately Stamp collecting

Prints

    Aquatint Engraving on copper using a resinous ground and nitric acid.

    Sugar aquatint Use of sugar with the above to get an effect of a positive brushstroke. More spontaneous feel to design.

    Copper and steel etching Use of steel needle on copper or steel plate – the latter is more for commercial use and gives a harder effect. All original engravings should have the imprint of the plate round the edges of the pictures, and be on the paper of the period.

Linocut   Design cut in relief on block of lino. Prints are obtained from this, several blocks being used for different colours. Linocuts usually show the texture of the tools used.

Lithograph   Drawing or painting on a thick slab of stone or zinc plate. For different colours, different stones or plates are used.

Silk screen prints   A combination of stencils and sometimes photography with silk screen frames. Parts which are not to take colour are masked with gummed tape. A versatile medium which does not require the use of machinery.

Wood engraving   Wood blocks used with wood-engraving tools. Thomas Bewick reproduced his drawings of animals and birds in this way.

Tempera   Method of painting on canvas, chalk, plaster or wood with colours mixed with egg yolk instead of oil.

Topography   Detailed representation, for example on maps, of natural and artificial features of a town or district.

Table of English monarchs

Anglo-Saxon

Early Saxon kings	978–1042
Edward the Confessor	
	1042–1066

Norman

William the Conqueror	
	1066–1087
William II	1087–1100
Henry I	1100–1135
Stephen	1135–1154

Plantagenet

Henry II	1154–1189
Richard I	1189–1199
John	1199–1216
Henry III	1216–1272
Edward I	1272–1307
Edward II	1307–1327
Edward III	1327–1377
Richard II	1377–1399

Lancaster

Henry IV	1399–1413
Henry V	1413–1422
Henry VI	1422–1461

York

Edward IV	1461–1483
Edward V	1483
Richard III	1483–1485

Tudor

Henry VII	1485–1509
Henry VIII	1509–1547
Edward VI	1547–1553
Mary I	1553–1558
Elizabeth I	1558–1603

Stuart

James I	1603–1625
Charles I	1625–1649
Commonwealth	1649–1660
Charles II	1660–1685
James II	1685–1688
William III and Mary II	
	1689–1702
Anne	1702–1714

Hanover

George I	1714–1727
George II	1727–1760
George III	1760–1820
George IV	1820–1830
William IV	1830–1837
Victoria	1837–1901

Saxe-Coburg Gotha

Edward VII	1901–1910

Windsor

George V	1910–1936
Edward VIII (uncrowned)	
	1936
George VI	1936–1953
Elizabeth II	1953–

Useful books

Antiques
Popular Antiques and Their Values, R. A. Curtis and M. J. Miller, Lyle
Antique Toys and Their Background, Gwen White, Batsford
The Encyclopedia of Furniture, Joseph Aronson, Batsford

Architecture
English Architecture at a Glance, Frederick Chatterton, Architectural
Press
A History of Architecture, Banister Fletcher, Athlone Press
The Architecture of England, Doreen Yarwood, Batsford

Costume
Costume Cavalcade, Henry Harald Henson, Methuen
Dictionary of Costume, R. Turner Wilcox, Batsford
English Costume from the Second Century BC to 1967,
Doreen Yarwood, Batsford
*Rural Costume: Its Origin and Development in Western Europe and the
British Isles*, Alma Oakes and Margot Hamilton Hill, Batsford

Crafts
The Technique of Woven Tapestry, Tadek Beutlich, Batsford
Art and Craft Today, Compiled by Henry Pluckrose, Evans
The Book of Crafts, Compiled by Henry Pluckrose, Evans
Introducing series and Art Technique series, Batsford

Embroidery
Fabric Pictures, Eugenie Alexander, Mills and Boon
Embroidery (published quarterly), Journal of the Embroiderers' Guild
Anchor Manual of Needlework, J. and P. Coats, Batsford
Inspiration for Embroidery, Constance Howard, Batsford
Samplers; Quilting; Patchwork, Averil Colby, Batsford

History
Larousse Encyclopedia of Ancient and Mediaeval History, Hamlyn
A History of Everyday Things in England, Volumes I to V, Marjorie
and C. H. B. Quenell, Batsford

English Life Series edited by Peter Quennell, Batsford
Everyday Life series, Batsford
Larousse Encyclopedia of Modern History, From 1500 to the present day, Hamlyn
A History of the British Commonwealth, K. Walker, Batsford

Museums
Museums and Galleries in Great Britain and Ireland (published annually), ABC travel guides Ltd

Paintings and Sculpture
Story of Art, E. H. Gombrich, Phaidon
European Painting and Sculpture, Eric Newton, Penguin

Poetry
Golden Treasury, Palgrave, Various publications

Teaching
Art for Young People, Eugenie Alexander and Bernard Carter, Mills and Boon
Film in Teaching, Keith Kennedy, Batsford
Photography in Art Teaching, Alan Kay, Batsford
Film Making in Schools, Douglas Lowndes, Batsford
Visual Awareness, Frederick Palmer, Batsford